easy to grow!
Flowers

Good Housekeeping

easy to grow!
Flowers

COLLINS & BROWN

First published in the United Kingdom in 2010 by
Collins & Brown
10 Southcombe Street
London
W14 0RA

An imprint of Anova Books Company Ltd

The Good Housekeeping website is
www.allboutyou.com/goodhousekeeping

10 9 8 7 6 5 4 3 2 1

ISBN 978-1-84340-539-9
A catalogue record for this book is available from the British Library.

Reproduction by Dot Gradations Ltd, UK
Printed and bound by Times Offset, Malaysia

This book can be ordered direct from the publisher at www.anovabooks.com

The following pictures are reproduced with kind permission of GAP picture library and Elke Borkowski, Zara Napier, Fiona Lea, JS Sira, Jerry Harpur, Martin Hughes-Jones, Clive Nichols, Jonathan Buckley, BBC Magazines Ltd, Tim Gainey, Lynn Keddie, Dave Zubraski, Neil Holmes, John Glover, Pernille Bergdahl, Marcus Harpur, Christina Bollen, Dianna Jazwinski, Richard Bloom: P.10; P.11; P.12; P.13(L,R); P.14(L); P.15(T,B); P.16(T,B); P.17; P.26; P.27(B); P.30; P.35(R); P.38; P.51; P.53(R); P.54(L); P.56; P.58; P.59(L); P.60; P.61; P.67; P.80; P.81; P.83; P.84(R); P.92; P.99(L); P.101; P.112(L,R); P.115(L); P.117.

Line illustrations on pages 20–21 drawn by Trina Dalziel.

Colour photography on the following pages by Lucinda Symons: P.18; P.19(L,R); P.22(L,R); P.23(all); P.24(BL,BM,BR); P.25(all); P.27(TL,TR); P.28; P.29(L,R); P.32(all); P.33(all); P.34; P.35(L); P.37(L,R).

The Publisher would like to thank Ginkgo Gardens for the kind use of their centre.

Contents

Basics

Tools and materials

Before you get started on your flower garden, you are going to need a basic set of tools. Always buy the best you can afford. Saving money on tools is a false economy. Choose those made from stainless steel with solid wood handles. Never buy unseen, try them out for size and comfort first.

It will make a big difference to your workload if your tools are comfortable to use. Take good care of them, as well. Clean off mud and soil after use and wipe them over with a cloth before putting them away. Service them regularly and sharpen them as necessary and they will last you for years.

Basic set

Spade: An essential tool, needed for heavy digging, breaking up clods, moving soil. They come in many different sizes and shapes, which is why you need to try them to find the one that suits you best. Make sure that the tread on the shoulders fits your foot comfortably, as well.

Fork: Used for loosening soil and breaking it down, especially after digging, and for lifting plants. The prongs are either round or flat – though if you are only buying one, the latter may be more useful as they do the minimum of damage to tubers when lifting plants.

Rake: Used for levelling soil, preparing seedbeds, removing stones and debris. Widths vary, but an 8 to 10-tooth rake is adequate for most purposes. It is very important to make sure the weight and balance are right for you, as it is difficult to work with one that is too heavy or cumbersome.

Hoe: You will need two types: the Dutch hoe, which has a flat rectangular blade that is used, as you walk backwards, to remove weeds, loosen soil or draw a drill; and the draw or swan-necked hoe, which has a blade at right angles to the handle. This is pulled towards you rather than pushed away, and is useful on heavier soils.

Hand trowel and fork: The trowel is a versatile tool, but is primarily used for planting. The fork is useful for weeding near plants and loosening soil. They need to be sturdy and well made. They come in different shapes and sizes, so take your time to find the one that is most comfortable for you.

Garden line: Essential for making sure your rows are straight when planting seeds. You can buy them, or make your own by tying twine to two short canes.

Cultivator: Not essential, but the three to five claw-like prongs are useful for breaking up ground and weeding between plants.

Mattock: This is a heavy chisel-bladed hoe, again not essential, but sometimes easier to use on hard ground.

Pocket knife: Invaluable for slitting open bags of compost or manure, cutting twine, taking cuttings, etc.

Sharpening stone: Useful to have to keep edges sharp and well maintained.

Secateurs/shears: For pruning, cutting, keeping things tidy.

Others

Watering can: Chose a sturdy one – plastic or metal – with a capacity of seven to nine litres (1½–2 gallons). You will need two detachable roses – one coarse and one fine – so you can match flow to plant.

Wheelbarrow: For moving large amounts of soil, manure, plants, bags, etc. Again, size and balance is personal and you may find a secondhand one does the job as well.

Bucket: For holding soil and liquid materials, or moving quantities of stuff around the plot.

Carrying sheet or bag: Keep nearby while working to

Hand tools
Good quality hand tools with solid wood handles make gardening much easier and last longer.

save time on trips to the compost heap or shed.

Bamboo canes: A selection of various sizes for marking out areas or positions, and providing support for plants, nets and wire.

Twine: For tying up branches, stems, canes, wires, etc.

Gloves: Choose a lighter, supple pair for pruning and planting, and a heavy duty pair for messier jobs such as handling prickly and stinging plants.

Horticultural fleece: To protect plants from the cold or pests, or to warm up the ground.

Cloches: A variety of different shapes, sizes and materials, including glass, plastic and polyurethane. For covering rows or individual plants – useful if you want to bring forward or extend the growing season, or for warming up the soil prior to sowing or planting.

Cold frames: Used for bringing on young plants or protecting a growing crop. They can be static with a solid floor, or movable (without a floor) to offer protection for plants growing in the ground, or adapted to make a hot bed.

For sowing seeds

Seed trays and small pots: Made of plastic (though wooden and terracotta types also available) and used for sowing seeds that need to be pricked out when they have germinated.

Modules: For sowing individual seeds to grow on to the planting out stage.

Biodegradable pots: Used for sowing crops that do not like their roots disturbed. Once the seedling is large enough to be planted out in the ground, the whole thing can go in and the container will rot down as the plant grows.

Dibber: A pointed metal or wooden tool used to make holes for planting seeds or young plants. A small one is used for pricking out seedlings.

Labels and markers: Essential so you know what is where. Many different types available in plastic, wood or slate with appropriate pencil or pen.

Propagator lids: Usually made of clear plastic and put over seed trays to speed up germination. You could also use cut-off plastic bottles set over individual pots.

Electric propagator: A small unit in which seeds are placed when a specific temperature is needed to germinate them (usually 13–16°C/55–61°F). The heat source may be a light bulb, heated plates or coils. Not essential, but a useful piece of equipment to have and they are usually inexpensive to run.

Types of flowers

Herbaceous perennials are what gardening is all about – flowers and colour. They are generally long-lived, resilient species that die back every autumn to re-emerge the following spring. At certain times of year they are accompanied by the riot of colour that spring and autumn bulbs bring and the multifarious delights of the many annuals and biennial plants that complete a garden display.

The seasonal growth habit of perennials gives them a strongly dynamic character – many being practically invisible over the winter, yet growing to over 2m (6½ft) by the end of the year. This creates a strong sense of change in the garden, quite different to one dominated by shrubs or conifers. Winter, when the majority are dormant, need not be dull, because many perennials have dead stems and seed heads that are attractive in a ghostly way, especially in low, winter light.

Perennials for colour

In many gardens it is shrubs and, perhaps, trees that make up the framework, with perennials being the 'infill'. Given that they take up relatively little space, and flower over a long period, it makes sense to rely on perennials for the bulk of the garden's floral interest. The perennial year starts off in late winter with a limited number of extremely versatile plants, with often strangely coloured flowers and attractive, evergreen leaves. While there are certainly a number of attractive, spring-flowering perennials and plenty of spring-flowering bulbs, it is not until early summer that perennials really get into their stride, with the pinks and blues of the hardy geraniums ('cranesbills').

Because perennials have to renew all their above-ground growth every year, it is not, perhaps, surprising that the majority flower later in the year. Numbers build up through mid-summer to a peak in late summer and early autumn. Mid-summer sees monardas in pinks, purples, and mauves, later months a huge variety of species from the daisy family, such as asters and rudbeckias. Yellow is the dominant late colour, although there are plenty of good blues and violets as well.

Using bulbs

Bulbs are nature's form of instant gardening, neatly packaged and able to spring to life within months. Plants have tended to evolve the bulb form as a way of surviving adverse conditions – they can either grow rapidly in spring, before trees overhead have sprouted leaves, or they can grow in hot, dry climates or mountain areas that have short growing seasons.

Cottage-style garden border
A perennial planting of cottage-style garden favourites – tall purple foxgloves (Digitalis) and white phlox, along with nigella and roses – is ideal for a country style garden.

Spring-flowering plants
There are few more pleasing sights in gardening than a magnificent display of spring bulbs in full bloom.

Many bulbs are still dug up from their native countries, resulting in losses and local extinction. Rarely do they do as well as cultivated ones, so ensure you buy from companies who can assure you that all their bulbs are cultivated and propagated in nurseries. Bulbs are invaluable for bringing spring colour to gardens and are very easy to combine with other plants. Plan ahead and you can have bulbs year-round!

Bulbs for all seasons

The bulb year starts with snowdrops, aconites and crocuses, which may be grown under trees or in grass.

Daffodils and narcissi come next, available in a great many varieties, both 'normal' size and dwarf. The larger daffodils are useful for 'naturalizing' in grass.

Wonderful shades of blue are very much a feature of spring bulbs. For example, crocuses are among those that come early in good blues, although they prefer sunnier conditions. Tulips tend to flower later, as spring turns into summer. As well as the vast range of brightly coloured, stiffly upright hybrids, there are a large number of 'species' tulips, which are the wild ancestors of the hybrids. These are much smaller and more informal in habit, but just as cheerfully coloured. Lilies (*Lilium spp.*) are probably the best-known summer bulbs.

At the end of the year, the smaller bulbs come into their own again, with cyclamen flowering beneath trees.

Places for bulbs

Bulbs can be planted underneath deciduous shrubs or around summer-flowering perennials to bring colour to what would otherwise be bare ground. Try combining them with early perennials like primulas, pulmonarias and hellebores.

It is important, however, not to plant them in places where they might get dug up accidentally during the summer. Smaller bulbs can be interplanted with dwarf shrubs and alpines in alpine gardens. Species tulips make excellent alpine-garden plants, and are good with alpines in containers, as well.

Bulbs easily become naturalized given the right conditions, which means that they spread themselves over the years. When they are grown in a lawn, it is important that the grass is not cut until the leaves have died back.

Buying bulbs

Buying bulbs is more fraught with problems than almost any other plant purchase. They are easily muddled for one thing, which makes buying them in prepacks from garden centres the most reliable way of getting what you want. These, however, often contain substandard bulbs. The punier the bulb, the less well it will flower. The best way of buying them is from a reputable mail-order company that specializes in bulbs.

Annuals and biennials

Annuals are plants that complete their life cycle within one year – germinating, flowering, setting seed and dying. Hardy annuals can withstand late frosts and so can be sown in the ground in spring without danger. Half-hardy annuals are frost-sensitive, so are usually started off inside and planted out once there is little risk of frost. These include a certain number of plants, such as ageratum, that are, in fact, perennials in frost-free climates. They are grown as annuals in cooler climates, since it is possible to bring them to flower from seed in only a few months. The half-hardies are often referred to as bedding plants. Biennials are plants that are started off as seed one year, to flower the next, either dying after flowering or being discarded. Hollyhocks (*Alcea spp.*) are an example.

Fillers and bedders

The speed with which annuals grow and the intensity of their colours are the main reason for their popularity with gardeners. They usually start to flower in mid-summer, after the perennials of early summer but

Shade-loving biennials
Although we often think of annuals and biennials as being plants only for sunny corners of the garden, some like the biennial foxglove (Digitalis) do best in partial shade and are ideal for adding colour to a shady spot in the garden or for woodland planting.

before the profusion of late-season perennials has started. For people wanting a practically instant garden, annuals are just what is needed.

Annuals are particularly useful in new gardens where there are considerable gaps between young plants. They provide temporary cover while you make your mind up about permanent plans.

In established gardens, annuals of either kind are ideal for combining with other plants as gap fillers among shrubs and perennials. They provide colour long after the shrubs and perennials have finished flowering, or, in the case of late perennials, before they have got into their stride. They can even be grown over dormant spring bulbs, provided there is no risk of the bulbs being uprooted when the annuals are removed at the end of the year.

While there are no true spring-flowering annuals available for gardens, there are certain plants, usually short-lived perennials, or biennials, that take their place as spring bedding, being discarded after they flower. These are generally started off as young plants, from seed, the year before and planted out in autumn or late winter. Pansies (Viola hybrids) are probably the best known.

Formal versus informal

There are two traditions of annual growing. One is the formal one, familiar from public parks the world over, with the emphasis on strong, contrasting colours and geometrical layouts, using a lot of half-hardy annuals. The other is the informal, cottage-garden tradition, which relies on cheaper hardy annuals that are sown where they are to grow. Here the colours are more muted, many are fragrant and a certain amount of untidiness is acceptable. Both traditions are currently undergoing changes since both are now using a much wider range of plants than formerly.

French marigolds (*Tagetes spp.*) and petunias are typical of the first tradition, while cornflowers (*Centaurea cyanus*) and pot marigolds (*Calendula officinalis*) are cottage garden staples.

Annuals in containers

Annuals, or plants grown as annuals, are a favourite for use in containers. Hanging baskets, tubs and window boxes are the most usual, but there is nothing to stop those imaginative gardeners who make use of practically anything that holds soil. Given that most have been bred for compactness and a long flowering season, it is the half-hardy annuals such as petunias and lobelias that often find their way into containers of all descriptions.

Just as foliage plants are used in the perennial border, so they can be used among annuals, too. Silver-leaved species are often found in hanging baskets, their foliage forming an attractive counterpoint to the flowers. Effective containers have a lot of plants packed into them, which means that the potting mix used must be very fertile. The best way to make sure that the plants never run short of nutrients is to use slow-release fertilizer pellets, which gradually release nutrients over the whole summer. Plentiful and regular watering is also essential.

When it comes to designing container plantings, a few plants widely used have more impact than trying to use as many as possible. The same 'rules' that apply to mixing colours and using structural plants in borders can be applied to containers as well.

Long-lasting displays
Annuals, especially those that are half-hardy, are favourites for window boxes (left) and containers (right), because many have been bred for their compactness and long flowering seasons.

Choosing plants

Harmony is perhaps the most important word in making a garden. You want somewhere that is relaxing but also stimulating to the senses, in which art and nature have reached a happy equilibrium. Creating a balance between the different elements of a garden, such as the paving, lawn, trees, shrubs and flowers, is crucial to the end result.

Colour is an essential element of all garden design, but because the growth cycles of flowers are relatively fleeting, it can be difficult to maintain interest year-round. The stronger the framework of the garden, with plenty of 'architectural' plants (those with strong and distinct shapes) to create visual interest, the less vital it will be to have flowers all the time.

Small gardens are especially difficult to plan, due to the constraints of space. All plants are highly visible, so there is no room in a small garden for the spectacular flowering plant that looks messy for the rest of the year. Good foliage and flowers with a long season are vital in situations such as these, together with careful, regular plant maintenance.

Creating a structure

It is the larger or more upright plants that do most to develop the garden framework, dividing it into sections and serving as a guide as you walk or look around. Trees or shrubs with a narrow, vertical, columnar habit have lots of impact, and are useful as they take up little space. Trees, under whose branches you can walk, hedges that act as green walls, or plants with strong shapes all provide the visual 'bones' for the garden. The softer, more formless shrubs and flowering perennials are the 'flesh'. Some of the most successful gardens are those that balance the formality of clearly designed shapes, such as clipped hedges and topiary, with the informality of burgeoning borders of flowers and shrubs.

Spring colour
An unusual, contrasting bedding design with magenta tulips and yellow wallflowers brings strong colour to the garden in spring.

Autumn foliage
A dramatic canopy of foliage can provide both colour and interest in the garden, as the contrasting golds of this *Liquidambar orientalis* and (behind) the reds of Japanese maple (*Acer palmatum* 'Osakazuki') demonstrate.

Year-round interest

Some gardeners are happy to have most of their garden flowering at once. They like to see a spring garden with lots of bulbs, or an early summer garden with roses and perennials, and they are happy to let it rest for the remainder of the year. Most gardeners, though, prefer to attempt a long season of interest, which involves trying to interweave plants so that there is always something, or some part, that looks good.

A garden takes time to develop, and never stands still. Planning planting for the short, medium and long term helps avoid the great gaps that can try the patience of even the most dedicated.

Harmony and contrast

Making a garden is an intensely personal business. What one person loves, another may hate. Such varying reactions are often to do with the level of harmony and contrast in the planting. Very harmonious gardens, where all the colours match, and clashes or surprises are avoided, are soothing, restful places. Those who like more stimulation may prefer gardens with lots of vivid, contrasting colours, or a wide and dramatic range of leaf shapes and plant forms.

Harmony in gardens is relatively easy to achieve with single colour schemes. 'White gardens' are particularly rewarding and straightforward. Plantings based on colour contrast are more difficult to get right, and are much more personal. Mixing strong colours can create results that are vibrant to some, but too obtrusive and clashing to others.

Organic gardening

You can also help to achieve harmony in your garden by working with nature to replenish its resources as you make use of them. You can do this by feeding the soil with plant waste such as decaying grass cuttings or autumn leaves that provide beneficial micro-organisms. This is what organic gardening is all about – growing fruit, vegetables, flowers or ornamental plants using plant matter, compost and beneficial insects rather than synthetic products such as pesticides and fertilizers.

Soft harmonies
The delicate blues, mauves and pinks and the softly billowing shapes of a herbaceous perennial border in summer are a study in gentle harmony.

Mixing colours and shapes
Big, bold shapes, such as this spiky, variegated agave, make a striking feature against softer planting.

15

PLANTS FOR SPECIFIC CONDITIONS

When you are creating your garden and planning your plantings, it is important to analyse the different conditions in various areas and then select and install suitable plants accordingly. What will grow well in full sun will not work in deep shade, and so on. Choose and buy your plants carefully.

Plants for dry sun
Many flowers like dry, sunny conditions. Tall purple alliums rise above pink aquilegias in this summer border.

Plants for shade
Many plants, such as euphorbia, thrive in shade or partial shade. (above).

Plants for particular situations

To make a successful garden it is crucial to choose plants that are suitable for the prevailing conditions. All plants have preferences: moist or dry soils, acidic or alkaline, warm climates or cold. Traditionally, gardeners have expended energy on making conditions suit particular plants, in places where they would not naturally grow, by changing the nature of the soil or by using copious quantities of water. However, water shortages and the pollutant effects of chemicals have compelled people to think in terms of a more natural approach. Instead of changing conditions to suit plants, today the trend is towards choosing plants to suit the place.

What grows best?

Before you select plants for your garden, it is advisable to learn as much as you can about the area in which you live, since this will determine what you can grow. A good way of finding out which plants will grow well is to visit local arboretums and gardens that are open to the public. An area where everyone seems to have rhododendrons means that you can grow these acid-lovers, too, as well as azaleas, camellias and many more.

Keep a notebook handy to record plants that you like and that thrive in gardens with similar conditions to yours. It is a good way of building up your own body of knowledge. Once you have a clear idea of what the area can or cannot offer, you will be in a position to select plants that will succeed with little effort on your part.

Climate is the place to start. Is your area one that regularly experiences cold winters or hot, dry summers? If it is, then the hardiness of plants or their drought tolerance are two important limiting factors. Then there is the 'micro-climate', which refers to factors that affect the overall climate on a small scale and of your garden in particular.

A wall or hedge that protects the garden from the prevailing wind may mean you are able to grow a range of more tender plants than anyone else in your neighbourhood. On the other hand, being in an exposed position, or in a frost hollow, where cold, heavy air gathers, can mean the opposite. Light is yet another very important factor. Is your garden shaded by trees, or is it on the sunless side of a hill or your house? If it is, then you need to concentrate your efforts on growing shade-tolerant plants.

The soil is the other major consideration. Is it generally damp or even wet, or is it very free-draining and so liable to dry out in summer? Is it fertile and is it acidic or alkaline? You may not require a soil-testing kit to find out – gardening neighbours can often supply the answers.

Hardiness rating

The hardier the plant, the lower the temperature that it will tolerate. In the following plant directory pages, plants that will not survive temperatures less than 5°C (40°F) are described as 'tender' – meaning they are not at all hardy – in individual entries. Other plants are hardier, and are given ratings as follows:
* Half-hardy: will survive 4 to -1°C (30–40°F)
** will survive -1 to -7°C (20–30°F)
*** will survive -7 to -17°C (0–20°F)
**** will survive -17 to -30°C (-20–0°F)

The temperatures given in the individual entries denote the optimum growing temperature range for the plant in question.

Choosing your plants

Any garden benefits from having a good mixture of plants, both in terms of height and shape, and in the variety of foliage and flower form and colour. While it is always preferable to have lots of flower colour, it is still possible to create much interest without it.

Plants for shady parts of the garden inevitably concentrate on their leaf form and shape; plants for full sun have more flower power. Make sure that you choose those that do well for these differing situations, and look, too, at the soil conditions. Some plants prefer acidic soil, others alkaline. Rhododendrons and azaleas, for example, grow very poorly on alkaline soil but on peaty soil they thrive and quickly provide useful ground cover for gardens. Hopefully, the differing habitats in your garden will allow you to choose a variety of plants from dry loving to damp loving, sun loving to shade loving.

Natural planting

The next time you visit the countryside or go on holiday, look at the plants around you. Notice how those that grow in exposed places usually have tiny, closely packed leaves, how those in hot, dry areas have a tendency to grey foliage or succulent leaves and how woodland plants are often evergreen or dormant in the summer. All these are adaptations that plants have evolved over millions of years to enable them to grow successfully in different environments.

It makes sense to take advantage of this, and select plants for our gardens that are naturally adapted to our particular type of soil and climate, whatever it is.

Gardeners often complain of bad drainage, or of dry, or clay, or alkaline soil. They never seem satisfied, and are prone to label anything that is not a perfect loam as a 'problem garden'. However, the fact is that nature has developed a wonderful and beautiful flora for every 'problem', at least those that are of natural origin.

A good start is to consider growing more wild plants native to your region. They are often very beautiful, but underrated for being wild, and at least they are perfectly adapted and will not have difficulty growing. If there are no local nurseries selling local wild plants, you can collect seed (but never dig up the plants) and propagate them yourself.

Natural planting
A woodland edge provides the ideal habitat for shade-loving perennials, including geraniums, ferns, and these foxgloves.

Preparing the site

When you dig, you are creating better growing conditions for your plants. Digging opens up the soil and lets in air, which allows organic matter to break down more easily and release nutrients. It also improves drainage and encourages plants to form deeper root systems. As you dig, you have the opportunity to add manure or compost to the soil and to remove perennial weeds, or to bury annual weeds and other plant debris. All will add nutrients to the soil.

As a general rule, autumn is the best time to dig, especially when you are clearing a patch of land or beginning cultivation for the first time. At this time of year the soil should be perfect for preparation, neither too wet nor too hard. Leave the soil roughly dug over the winter months, so that the frost and rain can break down the larger clods of earth and improve the soil texture. Never dig the ground when it is frozen or waterlogged, because this severely damages the soil structure.

There are three different digging techniques. In simple digging (see opposite) a spadeful of soil is lifted and inverted as it is dropped back into its original position. In single digging (see page 20) the soil is cultivated to the depth of one spade, using a trench system, and in double digging (see pages 20–21) the soil is cultivated to the depth of two spades, again working across a plot that has been divided into trenches. All have different purposes and have evolved over centuries.

HOW TO DIG

The depth of your topsoil, the quality of drainage in your garden and whether or not your plot has been previously cultivated, will all determine the best digging method to use. Single and double digging (see pages 20 and 21) are the most effective and labour-efficient digging techniques for areas of ground, but for a simple hole for planting, follow the sequence shown here. Before commencing any digging, make sure that the site is clear of all persistent weeds.

1 Dig a hole a few inches larger and deeper than the size of the container. Fork over the base of the hole to aid root penetration and drainage.

Simple digging

This is the easiest and quickest method for garden digging, good for clearing shallow-rooted weeds and creating a fine layer of soil on the surface. It is useful when digging in confined spaces and around mature, established plants.

No trench system is involved in this form of digging. Just lift a spadeful of soil and turn it over before dropping it back into its original position. Then break up the soil with the spade, in a brisk, chopping action. When the ground has been thoroughly dug over, leave it for at least three weeks before any planting or seed sowing is carried out. This will allow the soil plenty of time to settle and should be long enough for any buried weeds to be killed. The surface of the soil will begin to disintegrate and separate into smaller clods as it is broken down by the various actions of the weather. This will make it much easier to create a fine tilth on the surface later on, with the aid of a fork and a garden rake.

Using a fork

If the soil is particularly heavy and difficult to penetrate with a spade, it may be easier to use a fork, because the soil does not stick to the prongs in the same way that it does to a blade. Fork tines are ideal for breaking down the soil to a finer tilth, and teasing out unwanted plant roots and debris. However, in normal conditions, a spade is better for slicing through the soil and cutting through weeds.

The correct method

Many people dig incorrectly, with the doubly displeasing results that the soil is not properly cultivated and they risk back injury.

It is essential to adopt the correct posture and to use tools that are the right size and comfortable.

In the winter, make sure you are suitably dressed in warm clothes, since cold muscles are prone to injury. Do not dig too hard or for too long on the first occasion, and plan the order of work.

2 Tip the plant out of the container and place it in the hole, making sure the stem is at the same level in the ground as it was in the pot. Fill in the soil around the root ball.

3 Use your feet to firm down the soil, then water well. If the area is very dry, regular watering will be required for several weeks until the plant is established.

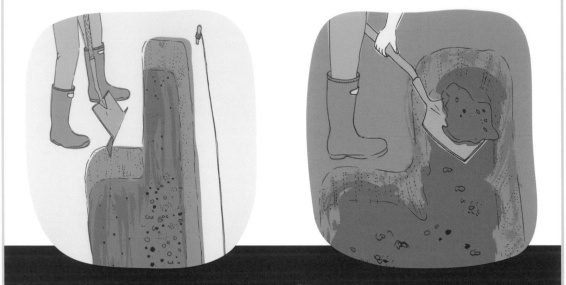

Digging trenches
Mark out the plot with garden lines. Dig trenches about 30cm (12in) wide and to the depth of the spade blade or fork tines.

Filling trenches
Fill each trench with the soil from the previous trench. For the last trench, use soil removed from the first.

Order of digging

Approach digging work systematically. Mark out the area to be dug with a taut garden line. Move the soil from the first trench to the end of the plot, ready to fill the final trench. Then fill each trench with soil from the next trench to be dug. If the plot seems too big, divide it in half and work each half in turn. This method avoids any unnecessary handling of the soil, which could compact it and possibly damage its structure.

Single digging

This method ensures that an area of ground is thoroughly dug to a consistent depth.

Single digging is usually done with a spade, but with heavier soils a fork can be used. The soil is cultivated to one spade's (or fork's) depth by digging progressive trenches across a plot.

First mark out a trench with a garden line. Dig a trench about 30cm (12in) wide and move the soil

from this first trench to the opposite end of the plot. Facing the trench that has already been dug, dig a second trench and use the soil from this trench to fill the first trench. Twist the spade or fork a little when putting the soil into the first trench so that the upper layers of the soil, and any weeds, fall to the bottom of the first trench.

Repeat the process down the plot. When the final trench is reached, it is filled with soil from the first trench. You can add manure or compost as you dig. Spread the manure around the trench and then fork it well into the soil.

Double digging

This is the deepest method of cultivation, and improves drainage by breaking up any hard pan which has formed in the lower levels of the soil. The trenches are twice as wide as for single digging and a spade and a fork are used.

How to double dig

Mark out, with a garden line, the area to be dug,
as with single digging.

1) Using the spade, dig a trench about 60cm (24in)
   wide and the depth of the spade blade. Then
   remove the soil to the opposite end of the digging
   area, ready to fill in the final trench.

2) Stand in the newly dug trench and break up the
   bottom soil, using a fork to the depth of its tines
   (see right). This cultivates the soil to a depth of
   about 50cm (20in). At this stage, add compost
   or manure, if needed, and fork it into the soil.

3) Mark out another trench, parallel to the first one. It is
   important to get these measurements accurate and to
   have each trench about the same size. They need to be
   roughly equal so that the same amount of soil is moved
   from trench to trench and the ground is kept roughly
   level. To make this easier, turn so that you are digging
   across the trench and divide it into three sections.

4) Dig the second trench, filling the first trench with
   the soil you have just excavated. Fork the bottom
   of the trench, as before, and continue to the next
   trench. Proceed in this way, methodically, across
   the plot. When you reach the final trench, fill it
   with the soil dug from the first trench.

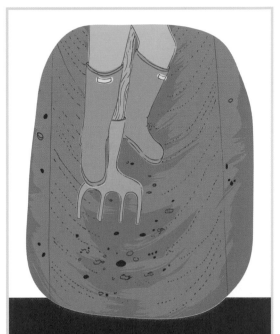

Double digging
Stand in each trench that has been dug and,
using a fork to the full depth of its tines, break
up the lower levels of soil to an overall depth
of 50cm (20in). This will improve drainage.

Sequence of work
Work across and then down the plot, as here, so that all of the ground is thoroughly dug.

21

Sowing seeds

Growing new plants from seed is the most common, and possibly the easiest, method of propagating a large number of plants quickly. It is ideal for growing plants for bedding displays and containers, and for filling gaps in summer borders. There is great variation between seeds, not only in terms of size and outer covering but also in the time it takes for them to germinate and their success rate.

What is a seed?

A seed is a complete plant in embryo, but it is in a resting phase. Certain seeds need preliminary treatment in order to speed up germination.

Pricking out

Seedlings raised in a nursery bed, such as hardy biennials and perennials, need to be transplanted to another nursery bed to grow on to a larger size before they are planted in their flowering positions.

As soon as they are about 5–8cm (2–3in) high and easily handled, carefully lift them with a hand fork, a few at a time to prevent the roots from drying out. They are replanted in rows spaced about 30cm (12in) apart, setting the plants about 15cm (6in) apart within the rows. Dig deep enough holes to allow the roots to dangle straight down, then return fine soil around them and firm it with your fingers. Plant them to the same depth that they were originally. After planting water them in thoroughly with a garden sprinkler or watering can fitted with a rose.

By the autumn of the same year you will have sizeable young plants for setting out in their flowering positions. The biennials will flower in the following spring or summer, and some of the perennials may also flower then, but others may need to grow a bit larger before they bloom. Lift and plant in the same way as seedlings, setting the plants at the appropriate distance apart.

PREPARING SEED

In order for your seeds to germinate successfully, some basic preparation prior to planting is a good idea. The seeds of various plants have different requirements – follow the instructions on the packet you buy – but generally one of the techniques demonstrated here will suffice.

Soaking seeds
To aid germination soak hard seeds in water to soften the seed coat.

Scraping seeds
Put small, hard seeds in a jar lined with sandpaper and shake the jar.

SOWING OUTDOORS

The seeds of hardy perennials and hardy annuals are normally sown out of doors. These seeds can be sown in their final flowering positions to avoid transplanting; most can be sown in spring, but some can be sown in autumn for an early start the following year. Check the sowing instructions on the seed packet. Make sure that the soil has warmed up; if it is cold, many seeds will rot.

Prepare the seedbed by digging well in autumn and adding organic matter at the rate of one cubic yard to every four square yards of soil. On heavy soils, incorporate grit or sand to open it up and improve drainage. A raised bed helps drainage, allowing the soil to warm up more quickly. Then sow the seeds as described in the steps below.

1 Tread the soil to form a firm surface. Use a rake to remove stones and make a level surface with a fine, crumbly texture.

2 Use a taut garden line for guidance on where to sow. Draw the corner of a rake or hoe along the soil to make a trench.

3 Sow seeds thinly in the trench, singly or in groups of two or three. Cover the seeds with a fine layer of soil using the rake.

4 Seeds can be watered in after sowing if a very fine spray is used. Alternatively, water the bed the day before you plan to start.

Low temperatures

Some seeds germinate only after exposure to low temperatures of 5°C (41°F) or less, in winter. Seeds will need to be sown in the autumn.

Sowing under protection

The seeds of more tender plants, such as half-hardy annuals and biennials, need artificial warmth, because they will not survive outside in areas where late spring frost occurs. Most of these seeds need temperatures of about 10–21°C (50–70°F) to germinate, but some need high temperatures. To raise the temperature and retain moisture, cover the newly sown seeds with a sheet of glass or with a plastic bag. Your seed packet will give exact instructions as to temperatures required.

Sow seeds in pots or seed trays. Plastic containers are the best, being easy to clean and sterilize.

Biodegradable containers are good for large seeds. The seeds are sown directly into a small pot or similar container where they germinate and grow until temperatures are right for planting out. Biodegradable

Germinating seeds
Place seeds in good light in warmth. Cress seedlings germinate very quickly in these conditions.

SEED VIABILITY

The length of time that seeds are viable – or capable of germination – varies. Some are viable for only one season. Most last for a year after harvesting, and many are viable for several years. Some (e.g. Paeonia) can take three years to germinate. If in doubt, check before proceeding further.

1 Fill the seed tray with a good seed compost. Firm the mix to within 1.5cm (¾in) of the top. Scatter fine and medium-sized seeds evenly.

2 If the seeds need dark conditions to germinate, sprinkle a thin layer of sieved soil over the top. Do not cover the seeds too deeply.

3 After carefully watering the seeds, leave to drain and cover the tray with a glass or plastic cover and place in a warm room.

SOWING LARGE SEEDS

Most large seeds can be sown in rows directly into the ground, but an alternative method is to plant them into a container. The majority of large seeds will be ready to sow straight from the packet, or they can be prepared as described on page 22.

1 For easier handling, sow large seeds in a container. Fill the pot with seed potting compost and level off the top.

2 To ensure that there are no air pockets in the soil, gently firm and level the mix with a flat-bottomed utensil, like a glass or a tamper.

3 Making sure there is a space between the top of the mix and the pot rim, sow the seeds evenly on the surface.

4 Cover the seed with a layer of mix if it needs darkness to germinate. Water the pot from below and cover it with glass.

containers are planted directly into the soil and eventually rot away. Follow instructions for the depth at which to sow seed. In general, if the seed needs dark to germinate (and not all seeds do) it should be covered with only its own depth of seed starter mix. Scatter fine and medium-sized seeds evenly over the seed starter mix. Spot sow larger seeds at regular intervals. Always label your seeds after growing.

Planting techniques

Plants that you have raised in the greenhouse or in an outdoor nursery bed, and those you have purchased from seed companies and the local garden centre, will eventually need to be planted out in their flowering positions. This needs to be done with a great amount of care, as the correct planting technique makes all the difference to subsequent growth and flowering. Poorly planted specimens may never become properly established and will fail to perform well.

Hardening off

Young plants that have been raised and grown on in a heated greenhouse, such as summer bedding plants, including all plug plants and larger young plants, must be gradually acclimatised to outdoor conditions before they are planted out, otherwise they will receive a severe check to growth. This technique, known as hardening off, is carried out in a cold frame.

Hardening off needs to start at least three weeks before planting out. Remember that frost-tender plants must not be planted out until danger of frost is over. If you don't have a cold frame, harden off young plants by taking them outside for longer and longer periods, before finally leaving them out overnight.

After putting the young plants in the cold frame, give a little ventilation for the first few days by opening the covers slightly during the day. Close the frame at night. Then over the next few weeks open the frame daily, gradually increasing the ventilation over this period by opening the covers more widely until fully open. But again, close the frame at night. A few days before planting out, the covers are left fully open at night also, provided there is no risk of frost.

It's important to keep an eye on your plants during the daytime as, if the cold frame is in direct sun, the temperature inside the small area can get very high, even in early spring. Young plants are very susceptible to drying out and wilting, even in a few hours.

Cold frames
Cold frames are smaller than greenhouses, aren't heated and can vary from large, brick-built structures to small, moveable ones. They are a halfway house before the plants are put in the ground and designed to keep the worst of the night cold or any frost off plants.

PLANTING A BULB

Bulbs need to be planted at roughly twice their own depth in order to flower successfully. Therefore, a bulb measuring 5cm (2in) deep should be planted at a depth of 10cm (4in). The depth of planting is important, because if bulbs are planted too close to the soil surface, or too deep, it will affect their flowering performance and/or their form. Tulips planted too close to the soil surface, for example, tend not to stand erect and to flop unattractively.

Spring-flowering bulbs are generally planted in the autumn, and summer- and autumn-flowering bulbs in early spring.

Bulbs are also very successful container plants, and can be grown in any good potting mix. They must be well watered, including during the period after flowering when next year's storage system for flowering is being built up.

If you plant bulbs in containers, remember to label the containers after planting. It is only too easy to forget precisely what you have planted!

1 Fill the container to the appropriate level with potting mix (using a layer of stones as drainage at the base) and place the bulb's growing point upward on top.

2 Top up with mix to within 2.5cm (1in) of the container rim. Water and keep moist but not wet, throughout the growing period, and after flowering.

Acclimatising plants
Young plants need to get used to the cold outside before they are put in the ground. If you don't have a cold frame put them outside during the day but bring them undercover into a cool place, like a garage, at night.

Planting out

When plants are fully hardened off they can be safely planted out. Let us first consider young plants in pots, seed trays, large-cell module trays and flexible-plastic or rigid polystyrene strips. The plants should be watered the evening before planting so that the compost is moist when they are planted out.

There are various techniques for removing plants from their containers but it must always be done carefully to avoid root disturbance as much as possible. Plants can be removed from pots by inverting the pot, placing one hand over the compost surface and tapping the pot rim on a hard surface, such as the edge of a bench. The rootball should slide out.

To remove plants from an ordinary seed tray, first tap the lower ends and sides on a hard surface to loosen the compost and, holding the tray close to the ground, gently throw the contents out. The compost should remain intact. Then the plants can be gently teased apart with your fingers. There will

be some root disturbance but this is inevitable. You can do the same with plants growing in strips.

Plants can be removed from module trays by pushing a pencil through the drainage hole in the base. This will loosen the plant, which can then be lifted out, without disturbing the rootball too much.

Plant immediately after removing plants from their containers to prevent the roots from drying out. Arrange the plants as required in the bed or border. Planting holes can be made with a hand trowel. Each hole should be large enough to take the rootball without squashing it, and should be of such a depth that after planting the compost surface is only slightly below soil level. Fill in around the plant with fine soil, making sure it is in close contact with the rootball and there are no air pockets, and firm it well with your fingers. To check whether it is firm enough, lightly tug the top of the plant — it should remain firm in the soil. The top of the rootball should be lightly covered with soil.

After planting 'tickle' the soil with a fork to remove any footprints and water in the plants if the soil is dry,

PLANTING GROUND COVER

The best way to plant ground cover is through woven black plastic, because this keeps weeds down until the plants are established. A large area may need a lot of plants, which can be very expensive. One answer is to propagate your own.

1 Peg down woven, black plastic across the area to be planted. Then cut crosses in the black plastic to create planting holes for the plants at appropriate distances apart.

ideally with a garden sprinkler or a watering can fitted with a rose.

Larger plants, such as herbaceous perennials bought in 12.5–15cm (5–6in) pots from the local garden centre, are planted in the same way as smaller potted plants. Some gardeners like to carefully tease out the outer roots before planting to help them establish quickly in the new soil. Just carefully pull out the roots with your fingers so that they are not growing in a circle around the soil ball. Again, set the plants so that the top of the rootball is only just below soil level.

You may also have larger plants of your own to plant, such as divisions of hardy perennials – large clumps of plants that you have divided or split into smaller portions for replanting. It is important to dig deep enough holes for these so that the roots are able to hang straight down without turning up at the ends.

Work fine soil between and around the roots and firm it well with your fingers. It is equally important to plant them at the same depth that they were originally. That is, with the crown of the plant,

where the growth buds are situated, at soil level. The buds must not be covered with soil as otherwise the crown may rot. If you are planting divisions of bearded irises, which produce thick rhizomes (swollen stems which grow above the soil), the rhizomes should sit on the soil surface, but the fibrous roots below should, of course, be under the soil.

Transplanting

For perennials and alpines raised in pots you have a choice of either potting up seedlings individually as soon as they are large enough to handle and growing them on outdoors or in an open cold frame, or you can line them out in nursery beds to grow on. If potting, start them off in 8cm (3in) pots and use well-drained, gritty, soil-based potting compost.

Seedling bulbs are best left in their pots for a further year to grow larger before being potted when they are dormant in their second year. Pot them to twice their own depth, say six to eight to a 12.5cm (5in) pot, using gritty soil-based potting compost.

2 Dig planting holes through the cut areas of the plastic. Carefully insert a plant through each cut area and backfill each hole. Water in well and keep watered in dry weather.

3 To disguise the black plastic, cover it with a layer of coarse bark chippings. Once the ground cover is well established and serving its purpose, you can remove the sheeting.

Propagation

It is both satisfying and economical to create beautiful displays in the garden by growing new plants from seeds and cuttings, or by dividing old, established clumps to form young, healthy plants. Many methods of propagation are very simple, once certain principles are grasped, and they require little equipment. Once you have gained some experience, a simple plant propagator and a cold frame will allow you to grow wonderful summer bedding displays and a much wider range of plants than is available in the garden centre. An added bonus is that you can easily swap plants with friends.

What is propagation?

Propagation is the term used to describe the processes by which seeds or other parts of living plants are managed in order to produce more plants. This process can be carried out in two ways – by seed or vegetatively.

Seed is a sexual method of reproduction in which the seed develops following the fertilization of the female part of the plant by male pollen. Vegetative propagation is an asexual method which includes taking cuttings of stem or leaf, dividing rootstock, layering or grafting in order to produce more plants.

Sowing seed (see page 22) is the easiest and most reliable method of producing large numbers of plants quickly. Plants grown from seed are also, generally speaking, healthier and more disease resistant.

Some plants, however, do not produce viable seed. The seeds may take a long time to reach flowering age, or do not breed true, which means that the seedlings can differ greatly from the parent plant in form, habit and flower colour. One advantage is that this variation allows many new and improved plants to be produced. However, in cases where an exact replica of the parent plant is desired – for example, in the propagation of especially fine forms of plants or of variegated plants – a vegetative method of propagation is used. This is the only way to be sure that any plant produced is identical in all its features to the parent plant.

Young cosmos plants
Growing new plants from seed is an easy, and inexpensive, way to increase plant stocks.

Choosing suitable plant material

Always choose cuttings or collect seed from the strongest and healthiest plants available to give the best possible chance of successful propagation.

Choose the best-formed fruits or seed heads and be aware that timing is critical when collecting seed. If you leave it too late, the seed will already have been dispersed, and if you gather seeds too early, they will not germinate. Gather seed on a dry day and if there is any dampness put them in the sun to dry thoroughly. If you are not sowing them immediately, store them in a cool, dry place out of direct sunlight. If you are buying seed, select packets which are undamaged and which have the most recent date stamp, because old seed does not germinate so well.

THE PROPAGATION ENVIRONMENT

Creating the right environment is the key to producing new plants. During propagation, plants are extremely vulnerable. It is therefore essential to provide a protected environment which reduces stress for the young plants and increases their chance of survival. Keeping seeds and seedlings in warm, humid conditions encourages rapid germination as well as healthy growth.

Leafy cuttings, when first taken, have no roots. To prevent them from wilting and encourage the speedy formation of new roots, they need to be in an environment with high humidity. This can be created very simply and cheaply by growing seeds on a warm windowsill, or by raising cuttings in a pot enclosed within a plastic bag. Hold the bag clear of the cuttings with sticks – the leaves will rot if they come into contact with the moisture that collects on the plastic.

The addition of bottom heat is necessary for the germination of certain seeds, such as half-hardy annuals, and for the successful rooting of some cuttings.

PROPAGATING EQUIPMENT

There is a range of propagating equipment available to suit any gardener's needs, from basic seed trays to cold frames and thermostatically controlled mist-propagation units.

A plastic plant propagator is useful for propagating seeds and cuttings in summer and there are units small enough to fit on a windowsill. Plant propagators with their own heat supply speed up rooting and germinating and are necessary for some seeds and cuttings.

Heated electric plant propagator
This plant incubator with room for three seed trays has an electric base with an adjustable thermostatic control for flexible temperatures. The rigid lid retains heat.

Containers
If you use ordinary plant containers for cuttings and some seeds you may have to cover them to make sure moisture is kept in at all times.

Take cuttings from thriving plants and discard any thin, weak shoots. It is best to choose non-flowering shoots, because these regenerate more readily than older or flowering shoots. If you have to take cuttings of flowering stems, remove any flowers so that all the energy goes into producing roots. Choose shoots from the current year's growth, because this is the most vigorous plant material.

Growing from cuttings

Increasing plants by taking cuttings from the stems is a common way to propagate woody plants. Stem cuttings are divided into three main types, according to the maturity of the plant and the time of year that the cuttings are taken.

Softwood cuttings are taken from shoots of the current season's growth as soon as a shoot's base starts to become firm, from late spring until late autumn.

Semiripe cuttings are taken from shoots of the current season's growth just as soon as the base of a shoot has turned woody, in late summer and autumn.

Hardwood cuttings are taken from fully mature shoots of the current season's growth of deciduous shrubs, trees and vines. They are cut from the parent plant immediately after their leaves have fallen, in late autumn and early winter.

Softwood cuttings

There should be minimal delay between removing a softwood cutting from the parent plant and potting it up, because immature stems are very prone to wilting.

Select a vigorous shoot on the parent plant and cut it 7.5–10cm (3–4in) long, with a sharp knife. Keep softwood cuttings in a closed plastic bag in the shade until you are ready to pot them up. Prepare each cutting by trimming the base and stripping away the lower leaves.

Dip just the base in rooting hormone powder and tap the cutting to shake off any excess. Insert at least 5cm (2in) of the stem into a soilless cutting compost. Water the pot thoroughly, ideally with sterilized water, preferably containing a fungicide. To prevent wilting, softwood cuttings should be kept in a well-lit, enclosed, damp environment while they grow roots.

1 Lift the plant and remove complete sections of root.

2 Cut the end of the root nearest to the plant straight across.

3 Cut the thinner end, nearest to the root tip, with a sloping cut.

4 Insert cuttings so the straight end is level with the mix.

HOW TO DIVIDE ROOTS

Propagating from pieces of root is a good technique for certain hardy perennials, including those that do not lend themselves to division. Plants that are often propagated from root cuttings include acanthus, globe thistle (echinops), Japanese anemones, mulleins (verbascums), oriental poppies (*Papaver orientale* cultivars), pasque flower (pulsatilla), border phlox, drumstick primrose (*Primula denticulata*) and sea holly (eryngium).

5 Cover with moist sand to stop the cuttings drying out.

Semiripe cuttings

Semiripe cuttings are propagated in a similar way to softwood cuttings, but at a later time of year. The stems of semiripe cuttings are therefore harder and more resilient than softwood cuttings. Potting up quickly is not quite so critical, because the cuttings will not wilt as quickly as softwood cuttings. Semiripe cuttings do, however, take longer to grow roots and there are various techniques that are adopted to improve rooting. Unlike softwood cuttings, any soft, sappy growth should be removed from the tip of a semiripe cutting before it is inserted into the cutting compost. Cuttings should be placed in a plant propagator or other closed environment while they produce roots. Semiripe cuttings, taken in autumn, can be allowed to root slowly over winter in a cold frame.

Hardwood cuttings

Hardwood cuttings can be taken at any time in late autumn and winter, but those taken before the cutting is fully dormant, in late autumn, are likely to be the most successful. They are planted outdoors and because the soil is moist and relatively warm, they have a chance to produce small roots before the onset of winter and should start into stem growth by mid-spring. Select a healthy shoot, 23–60cm (9–24in) long, from the current season's growth of the parent plant. Cut it straight across the bottom of the stem with sharp hand pruners. Cut the tip at an angle (but if the buds are arranged opposite each other, as in buddleja, make a straight cut).

In a well-cultivated part of the garden, make a series of holes for the cuttings by pushing the tines of a garden fork 15cm (6in) into the soil. Insert one cutting into each hole, so that it presses into the bottom. At least two-thirds of the cutting should be in the ground. Rake the soil around the cuttings and press it firmly around them. If conditions are dry, finish by watering the soil well. Then leave the cuttings to grow.

Division

You can increase most perennials by splitting a clump of plants, complete with roots and growth buds, into small sections, each of which grows into a new plant, identical to the parent. Either plant the divisions straight into their new site, or into spare ground until they are ready to be planted out permanently. You can rejuvenate many perennials in this way every 3–4 years. Division is best carried out when plants are semi-dormant and the soil is workable. Early spring is the main season.

Plants with fleshy roots, such as hostas, need to be cut with a sharp knife into sections, ensuring that each has its own roots and growth buds. Carefully cut away and discard any old and rotten portions of the roots. Replant divisions immediately in well-prepared soil, and water them with a fungicidal solution to prevent them from rotting. Plants with fibrous roots can be divided by easing the roots apart with your fingers or a knife. If the roots are too tough, you can split them into manageable sections with a garden fork. Replant immediately after division.

HOW TO DIVIDE PLANTS

Depending on the size and toughness of the plant, there are various methods that can be used to divide roots. Care should always be taken to be as gentle as possible so that minimum damage is caused.

1 Prise apart soft and fleshy roots using your fingers.

2 Tougher roots may require the use of a sharp knife.

3 Use a garden fork on bigger plants with tough roots.

Watering

Water is essential for all plant growth, although some plants have adapted to drought conditions and need very little moisture in order to survive. If you live in a climate with low rainfall it is important to choose plants that will tolerate dry conditions, unless you are able to spend time and thought on watering systems. Roof gardens and other sites exposed to drying winds increase the watering needs of your plants.

A variety of watering systems and devices are available to help you in your gardening, notably drip-watering systems and water-retaining granules. It is best to water at dawn or dusk when the sun's rays are less powerful and the evaporation rate is much reduced. To encourage deep roots to develop, water thoroughly and regularly rather than little and often.

Easy-watering systems

In any garden, easy access to water is essential, as many plants will require regular watering. An outdoor tap is vital, unless the kitchen tap is easily accessible. Also essential is a hose that is long enough to reach the farthest corners of the garden.

In times of drought, however, water may be rationed and you may well have to recycle washing water from the house. Installing a water barrel to collect runoff rainwater is a sensible precaution.

There are some simple systems available which deliver water to the garden, as needed, at the flick of a switch. If you have a small garden in a warm climate, or if you garden on an exposed site, such as a roof terrace, consider planning a soaker hose or drip-feed system, which can be laid permanently in the planting areas.

Drip-feed system

This consists of a series of fine bore pipes, with drip heads at intervals, that you can position exactly where water is required – at the foot of plants needing

HOW TO WATER CONTAINERS

Plants in containers lose water very rapidly through evaporation. Terracotta pots especially are notoriously poor at retaining moisture. Hanging baskets, with their small amount of soil and large area exposed to the elements, are very greedy for water and may well need watering once a day in hot weather. Group containers together to preserve moisture, and put them in shade in hot weather.

Watering the root base
To make sure water penetrates the potting compost thoroughly, make a few holes around the edge of the pot with a cane before watering.

frequent watering, for example. A soil-moisture detector can be fitted to the system, ensuring that the automatic system is overridden if the ground is sufficiently damp. Drip-feed systems tend to get blocked with debris, so it is important to clean the system regularly.

Leaky-pipe hose system

This is useful for watering large areas, such as awns, or for planted beds. It is an efficient way of using water, because it is directed straight at the roots. The hose is punctured with a series of fine holes so that a regular, even supply of water is delivered over the length of the hose. A similar system uses a porous hose. The system can be buried beneath the soil to make it both permanent and unobtrusive.

Retaining moisture

A major difficulty with growing plants in containers is keeping the plants supplied with water, especially when using soilless potting composts, because these are very difficult to re-wet after drying out. To overcome this, add granules of polymer to the mix. When wetted, these granules swell to form a moisture-retaining gel which can hold vast amounts of water. The water is gradually released into the mix.

Making the most of water

There are various ways to reduce the need for watering. Firstly, you need to increase the moisture-retaining properties of the soil, if it is sandy, by adding plenty of organic matter. Secondly, you need to reduce the amount of water lost through evaporation, by screening your plants from the effects of drying winds.

If your flowers are in containers, grouping plants together helps to reduce evaporation, as does using pebbles or stones over the soil surface.

Drought-resistant plants

If you live in a very dry climate with free-draining soil, you need to make sure your plants are as drought-resistant as possible, to give the plants the best chance of success. This will save you from spending a great deal of time watering. Generally speaking, apart from those succulent plants which store water in their tissue (either in their leaves or stem), plants that are tolerant of drought can be recognized by their foliage. It is usually silver-grey, finely divided, and sometimes covered in fine hairs or felt – all of which reduce evaporation.

Reviving a wilting plant
If a plant is wilting from lack of water, plunge it into a bowl of water so that the pot is covered. Leave it until air bubbles subside.

Watering hanging baskets
Hanging baskets dry out very quickly. Always soak the basket so the water runs out from the bottom and all the compost is wet.

Feeding

In order to grow well, plants need a balanced diet of nutrients. Nitrogen, phosphorus and potassium are the foods plants must have in large amounts to sustain a good growth rate. Nitrogen is needed for healthy growth and leaves, phosphorus is essential for good root development and potassium ensures both healthy flowers and fruits as well as disease resistance.

As a gardener, you should supply your plants with these nutrients in various forms depending on the circumstances. Some forms are particularly useful for conditioning the soil, others for supplying a direct source of food to the plant itself. Quantities of nutrients required depend on how intensively the garden is cultivated: closely packed vegetables require a great deal; shrub borders much less. Fertilizers contain plant nutrients in a concentrated form and are used in fairly small quantities. Manures are bulky and need to be added to the soil in large amounts – but they provide only a small quantity of nutrients. However, they do add valuable fibre, which is converted into humus to condition the soil. This also increases the activity of beneficial micro-organisms.

Composting animal manure
Animal manure is one of the best soil conditioners because it improves soil texture and provides some nutrients while the straw provides bulk. Compost manure for at least six months before adding it to the soil.

Fertilizers

These may be organic or inorganic in their origin. Organic fertilizers consist of dead plant or animal matter that has been processed, such as bonemeal, dried blood and fishmeal. They do not scorch foliage and are natural products. Inorganic fertilizers, also known as artificial, chemical or synthetic fertilizers, are derived from mineral deposits or manufactured by an industrial process. These are highly concentrated and faster-acting than organic types, but you must not exceed the dosage, or plants may be scorched or damaged.

Fertilizers can be applied in dried form or dissolved in water, as in liquid fertilizer.

Soil conditioners

Digging in quantities of bulky, organic matter introduces both nutrients and fibre into a garden soil.

Woody and fibrous material opens up heavy soils and improves the soil structure. It provides materials that improve moisture retention on lighter soils. Fibrous conditioners of this kind are ideal if long-term soil improvement is the ultimate aim. When they decompose they contribute to the formation of humus which absorbs other nutrients applied to the soil. Lime, while not a food, is also used to condition the soil. Never apply lime to the soil at the same time as fertilizers and manures.

Green manure

Organic matter can be added to the soil by growing a fast-maturing crop as temporary ground cover on a

APPLYING LIQUID FERTILIZERS

Liquid is usually easier and safer to apply than dry fertilizer, and the plant's response is often more rapid. The concentrated fertilizer is diluted in water. It is applied either to the soil or to the leaves, depending on the type. Mix the fertilizer thoroughly with the water before application, to reduce the chance of damaging the plants. Do not apply when rain is forecast, or it may be washed through the soil away from the plant's roots.

1 Dilute liquid fertilizers with water and apply with a watering can or a hose. These fast-acting fertilizers are useful for correcting nutritional deficiencies.

2 Apply liquid fertilizers as a foliar fertilizer or directly to the soil around the base of a plant. Most foliar fertilizers are soil-acting as well so runoff is absorbed by the roots.

bed that is empty for a while, usually over the winter. The crop is dug into the topsoil 6–8 weeks after germinating. This fast-maturing crop is known as a green manure and it is a means of improving both organic matter and nitrogen levels. The release of nitrogen is quite swift and so provides an early boost to plant growth. The greener and younger the manure, the less fibre is produced.

Dry fertilizers

These are nutrients in a dry, solid form – granules and pellets. They are mixed together and coated with a wax or resin compound which slowly dissolves and releases fertilizers into the soil. The release can take 6–18 months, depending on the thickness of the outer coating, soil moisture, temperature and pH. Apply these fertilizers by sprinkling them evenly over the soil and mixing them into the top layer with a fork. If the soil is dry, water the area after application to dissolve the fertilizer and wash it down to the root zone. An even distribution of fertilizer is essential, because damage to plants may occur if too much is used. Mark out the area you intend to fertilize into squares with canes and garden lines and then take care to sprinkle and spread the fertilizer as evenly as possible.

Fertilizing container-grown plants

To promote balanced and healthy growth in containers, use brand-name potting composts that contain measured amounts of fertilizer.

Additional fertilizers can be given if necessary by applying quick-acting fertilizers as a top-dressing, or by using foliar fertilizer or fertilizer spikes.

Mulching

A weed is any plant growing in a place where it is not wanted. Many weeds cause problems just because they are so tough and versatile that they can adapt to a wide range of growing conditions. For this reason they must always be dealt with before they get out of control. The most effective way to prevent them from appearing in the first place is to use a mulch.

Mulching for weed control

Mulching is the practice of covering the soil around plants with a layer of material to block out the light and help trap moisture. In today's gardens, where plastics are commonplace, inorganic (non-biodegradable) black plastic sheeting is often chosen. Though not inviting to look at, it can be hidden beneath a thin layer of more attractive organic (natural and biodegradable) mulch.

As a general rule, organic mulches provide the bonus of improving the fertility of the soil, but inorganic mulches are more effective because they form a better weed barrier. To be fully effective as a barrier, organic mulches must be applied as a layer at least 10cm (4in) thick. Both organic and inorganic mulches tend to be less effective against established perennial weeds, unless an entire area can be sealed until the weeds have died out and planting is carried out through the mulch while it is in place. One way of clearing weedy ground in summer is to cover the soil with a mulch of clear or white plastic, sealed around the edges. Weeds are gradually killed by a combination of high temperatures and lack of carbon dioxide.

The plastic sheeting can be removed after a time and used elsewhere. The treated area is weed-free, ready to plant and cover with an organic mulch, such as shredded bark or gravel (see below).

Gravel mulch
Covering the soil with a mulch such as gravel will block out light and prevent weed seeds from germinating.

Weeding

Weeds compete directly with your garden plants for light, nutrients and water. They can also act as hosts to pests and diseases (see pages 42–3), which can spread as the season progresses. Groundsel, for instance, often harbours the fungal diseases rust and mildew, and sap-sucking aphids. Chickweed also plays host to aphids as well as red spider mites.

Perennial weeds

Digging up perennial weeds is an effective disposal system, provided that every bit of the root system is removed from the soil. If only a few weeds are present, try digging them out with a knife or trowel, but you must remove the top 5cm (2in) of root close to the surface, to prevent the weed from re-growing. This method can be used in the lawn to get rid of individual or small patches of weeds, and is a reliable means of eradicating weeds growing close to garden plants. In this situation, often no other weed control method would be effective without risking damage to plants growing nearby.

Clearing weeds

The simplest way to deal with weeds is to remove them physically, either by pulling or digging them out or, if they are small, hoeing them off at soil level.

The biggest problem with this method of control is that most weed seeds require exposure to light before they germinate. Often, when weeding disturbs the soil, more air is allowed into the surface layers and an ideal seedbed is created. Although the existing weed seedlings are destroyed, the weed growth cycle starts all over again. This problem is often worse when using rotovators, because they leave the surface layers of soil light and fluffy, making a perfect seedbed. Perennial weeds are increased, too, because they are chopped into pieces, each capable of growing.

The most effective way to clear weeds, especially established perennials, is to use a combination of cultural and chemical methods. Spray weeds in full growth with a chemical herbicide and, as they start to die, bury them when the area is dug over. When the new weed seedlings germinate, spray them with a chemical while they are most vulnerable.

Annual weeds

Clearing annual weeds with a hoe is quick and effective, but the timing is important. The hoeing must be done when the weeds are tiny and before they start producing seed.

Hoeing will sever the stems of young weeds from the root system just below soil level. This both prevents the stem from forming new roots and stops the roots from producing a new stem. When hoeing, make sure you always walk backwards to avoid treading weeds back into the soil.

There is an old saying, 'One year's seeds make seven years' weeds', which has now been endorsed by scientific research and proved to be remarkably accurate – unfortunately for gardeners.

Annual weeds are capable of producing a staggering total of 60,000 viable seeds per square metre, per year. The vast majority of these seeds are found in the uppermost 5cm (2in) of soil, but they will usually germinate only when exposed to sufficient light levels. This is why mulching (see opposite page), which covers the soil and blocks out light, has become such a widely popular method of weed control. The added benefit of mulching is that there is also little chance of contaminating the soil with chemical residue.

General care

With some additional care, various plants can be made to flower longer, some tender kinds can be kept for a number of years and hardy kinds can be encouraged to remain young and vigorous, as well as ensuring that borders and beds remain neat and tidy at all times.

Dead heading

The removal of dead flower heads helps to ensure a neat and tidy appearance, and also encourages some plants to flower for a longer period. This applies especially to annuals and tender perennials, but also to some hardy perennials – for example, delphiniums and lupins may well produce a second flush of flowers later in the summer if dead blooms are removed.

Dead flower heads are usually cut off with some of the flower stem attached, using secateurs or flower scissors. With others, such as marigolds (tagetes) and pelargoniums, the dead blooms are easily snapped off between finger and thumb, thus speeding up the process. You may be able to use garden shears for plants that produce masses of very small flowers.

Remember that the dead flower heads of some hardy perennials look attractive over winter and can therefore be left until they become tatty in early spring. Examples are the flat-headed stonecrops (sedums) and achilleas, and ornamental grasses including miscanthus.

Over-wintering plants

Many tender plants used for summer bedding or containers can be kept from year to year, by rescuing them before or when the frosts start in autumn. For example, tender perennials such as pelargoniums, fuchsias and osteospermums can be propagated from cuttings in late summer or early autumn and the resultant young plants are wintered in a cool but frost-free greenhouse. The parent plants are lifted and discarded as they will probably be too big to store under glass and in any case young plants are best

for replanting. Tender winter-dormant tubers such as dahlias, cannas and tuberous begonias are lifted, cut down and stored in boxes of peat substitute in a cool, frost-free place over winter.

Annuals, whether tender or hardy, are pulled up and discarded when frosts start in autumn, as they cannot be kept from year to year, although you may be able to save the seeds for sowing in spring.

Renovating borders

Borders or beds devoted to hardy perennials, or parts of the borders where perennials are grown, need renovating every three to four years. This allows for improvement of the soil by digging and manuring, and if necessary the removal of any perennials weeds that have become established.

Border renovation also enables plants to be rejuvenated. The plants are lifted and heeled in on a spare piece of ground while the border is being dug. Then the large clumps of plants are split or divided into smaller portions, using the younger, more vigorous parts around the outside edge for replanting. The older centre part, which is declining in vigour, is discarded.

Borders and beds can be dug in the autumn and the plants split and replanted in early spring of the following year, or the whole operation can be undertaken in early spring if that is more convenient.

Supporting plants

Fortunately the majority of perennials and other plants are self-supporting, but there are some with weak or thin stems, or with heavy flowers, that will need artificial supports to stop them being flattened by wind and rain. Climbing plants such as honeysuckle or passionflower must also have supports.

Thin- or weak-stemmed hardy perennials, especially if they are tall such as some cultivars of Michaelmas daisy (aster) and bellflower (campanula), can be supported with twiggy hazel or birch sticks pushed in around and among them as they are starting into growth. Tall multi-stemmed annuals can be supported in the same way. Alternatively, metal plant supports which link together around the plant, forming the size required, are very effective.

Single bamboo canes can be used for tall annuals with single stems, such as sunflowers (helianthus). Heavy plants such as dahlias are best supported with a single wooden stake, about 2.5cm (1in) square, tying each stem to it as it grows. Support each stem of a delphinium with a single bamboo cane.

Make sure all supports are shorter than the flowering height of the plants and tie in stems loosely with soft garden string.

Climbing annuals such as sweet peas can be grown up a wigwam formed of bamboo canes. Alternatively, use an obelisk. Various kinds are available, including smart metal versions or more rustic ones made from willow or hazel. Some are suitable for patio tubs. Climbers can be supported on walls or fences with trellis panels fixed to the structure. Annual climbers can also be grown through larger plants such as shrubs.

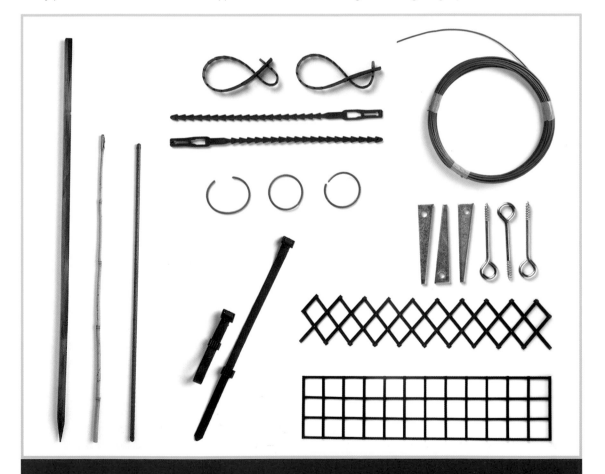

Types of support
Most flowers do not require support, but some taller perennials with weak stems or large, heavy flowers will benefit from staking or other support with anything from a bamboo cane to an obelisk made of willow.

Pests and diseases

These are the major pests, diseases and other problems that affect flowers. However, do not be alarmed, as although there are numerous things to be concerned about, your plants are unlikely to be troubled by all of these. For proven environmental reasons, there is a strong emphasis in these pages on non-chemical methods of control of the pests and diseases discussed.

Aphids

These are among the most troublesome of insect pests, particularly greenfly and blackfly, and they attack a wide range of flowers. Wash off aphids with plain or soapy water, or spray with insecticidal soap if necessary.

Black root rot

A disease affecting many flowers. The roots become black, but above-ground symptoms are yellowing and wilting leaves. Scrap sickly looking plants and plant something different in the affected site.

Bulb aphids

Certain aphids winter on bulbs and corms in store. Look out for them on crocuses, gladioli, lilies and tulips especially, and simply rub them off.

Bulb and corm rot

Bulbs of various kinds, including daffodils, lilies and tulips, are prone to rotting in store, caused by various diseases. Check for soft spots, particularly at the base of the bulbs (basal rot). Remove and discard rotting bulbs. Similarly, corms such as crocuses and gladioli are prone to several kinds of rot while in store, so check regularly and remove and discard any that show signs of rot.

Caterpillars

The caterpillars of various moths and butterflies eat holes in the leaves of numerous perennials and annuals. They are generally green, brown or grey and are generally hairy. Caterpillars are easily picked off and destroyed, or plants can be sprayed with an insecticide if necessary.

Cutworms

These caterpillars, the larvae of several different moths and greenish brown or greyish brown in colour, live in the soil and feed on roots and stem bases of plants, causing young plants to wilt and die. Remove any found during soil cultivations.

Damping off

This disease affects seedlings indoors, causing them to suddenly collapse and die. Damping off can spread rapidly and should be prevented by using sterilised compost and clean containers.

Earwigs

These night-feeding insects, easily recognised by their rear pincers, eat holes in flowers, buds and leaves. Remove and destroy any pests. Spray plants with an insecticide if necessary.

Foot rot

This disease causes the bases of stems to turn black and rot. Pull up and discard any plants that show signs of infection.

Grey mould

This major fungal disease, also known as botrytis, can infect all top growth of plants – flowers, buds, leaves and stems – resulting in rotting. Cut off any affected parts of plants, back to healthy tissue.

Leaf spot

Many diseases show up as brown or black spots on the leaves of numerous ornamental plants. The spots vary in size and some are in the form of rings. The best control method is to pick off any leaves showing spots. Spray affected plants with fungicide if necessary.

Mildew

The most common is powdery mildew, appearing as white powdery patches on the leaves of many plants. Remove affected leaves. Spray plants with fungicide if necessary.

Petal blight

This disease attacks chrysanthemums, and sometimes other related plants, and anemones, showing as watery lesions or brown spots on the petals. Remove affected flowers. Spray plants with fungicide if necessary.

Red spider mite

There are several kinds of these microscopic spider-like creatures that feed by sucking the sap from the leaves of many plants, particularly under glass. This results in fine pale yellow mottling on the upper leaf surfaces. Spraying plants regularly with plain water will deter the mites. Or spray plants with insecticidal soap if necessary.

Rhizome rot

This bacterial disease causes the leaves of rhizomatous irises to turn yellow and wither. Dig up and discard badly affected plants. Avoid damaging surrounding plants as you do this.

Rust

This fungal disease shows as rust coloured, orange, yellow or dark brown raised spots on the leaves and stems. Affected leaves should be removed. Spray with a fungicide if necessary.

Slugs and snails

Slugs and snails eat the leaves of a wide range of plants and also damage soft young stems and even flowers. Control by placing slug pellets around plants. Alternatively, remove them by hand.

Stem rot

Numerous diseases, but particularly sclerotinia, cause the stems of various perennials and annuals to rot. As there is no cure, plants that are badly affected should be removed and discarded.

Tuber rot

A fungal disease may attack dahlias in store, causing the tubers to rot. Check stored tubers regularly and if rotting is noticed cut it away to healthy tissue.

Viruses

Viruses are types of diseases that infect a wide range of plants. The most common symptoms are stunted and distorted plants. There is no cure: pull up and burn affected plants.

Weevils

These beetles are easily recognised by their elongated 'snout'. Their larvae are the main problem. Their feeding causes wilting, and invariably death in severe attacks. Use biological control with a pathogenic nematode in late summer.

Wilting leaves

Apart from wilting caused by various pests and diseases, the most common cause is drought. Young plants may never recover, even if watering is carried out. Make sure the soil never dries out, ideally by mulching permanent plants and by watering as necessary.

Woodlice

These pests feed at night and hide in dark places during the day. Physical control is not practical, except to ensure that any plant debris is not left lying around.

Annuals & Biennials

Ageratum houstonianum
Flossflower

Flowering from early summer onwards, this beautiful half-hardy annual has flower heads which resemble small powder puffs. Shown to their best when edging a formal bedding scheme, they are also good subjects for window boxes and containers.

Use the F1 hybrids now available; these give larger and longer trusses of blooms. The cultivar 'Adriatic' is in this class: its height is 20cm (8in), and the mid-blue flower is produced above light green hairy leaves. Although most cultivars are in the blue range, there are a few whites available.

Care
Flossflower will grow in most ordinary types of soil and tolerates all positions except heavy shade. Avoid planting out too early.

New plants
Sow seed in trays of seed compost in spring, under glass. When large enough to handle, prick out in the usual way. Plant out in final positions at the end of spring or when the risk of frost has disappeared. Until planting out, try to maintain a temperature of 10–16°C (50–60°F); lower than this will tend to check growth.

H & S 30 x 30cm (12 x 12in)

18–20°C (65–70°F)

Direct sunlight

Amaranthus caudatus

Love-lies-bleeding

This hardy annual has long, tail-like clusters of crimson flowers which can reach 45cm (18in) in length. The flowers are produced on stems up to 105cm (42in) tall. Leaves are ovate in shape and green in colour, the green changing to bronze as the season progresses. A. caudatus is used mainly in formal beds as a 'spot' plant to give height. Try them as individual specimens in largish containers or in groups in a mixed border. The long tassel flowers will appear in summer.

Raise plants for containers and formal borders by sowing in trays of good seed compost in early spring.

Prick off into individual pots under glass and plant out into their final positions in late spring.

Care
Love-lies-bleeding likes a well-cultivated soil in a sunny location. Keep plants well watered in dry periods.

New plants
For borders, sow the seed directly into the open ground in a sunny position in spring. When thinning out seedlings, give plenty of room for development – about 60cm (24in) apart.

H 100cm (39in)
S 45cm (18in)

16–18°C
(62–64°F)

Direct
sunlight

Althaea rosea
Hollyhock

The hollyhock was introduced from China in the 16th century. It comes in a diverse range of flower colours, from white and the palest shades to rich reds, pinks and a deep purple-black. There are also double forms. It is a stately plant that looks good, and grows best, against a wall. Hollyhocks love good drainage and thrive in brick and lime rubble.

In suitable conditions hollyhock self-seeds readily. It is this random seeding that produces the groups of hollyhocks with flowers of different shades that are so appealing.

Hollyhock has similar medicinal properties to *A. officinalis*. The flowers were used as a tisane to treat chest complaints, or as a mouthwash.

Care
Hollyhocks like well-drained soil and a site in full sun.

New plants
Sow seeds in spring or late summer directly into the border; this plant self-seeds.

Other varieties and species
A. rosea 'Chater's Double'; *A. r.* 'Summer Carnival'; *A. holdreichii*; *A. pallida*.

Borago officinalis
Borage

Borage has long been grown in herb gardens and is a firm favourite because of its beautiful intense blue, star-like flowers.

Borage self-seeds readily and in good soil forms a substantial plant. If you keep bees, it is worth seeding a large patch, since it will flower for months and bees love it. Borage will grow well in a container of rich soil, but will need frequent watering in hot weather.

Borage leaves impart a fresh cucumber flavour to summer drinks and should be used in fruit cups and wine cups. The young leaves make a delicious addition to a green salad, and the flowers look spectacular sprinkled over the top. The flowers can also be candied. Wonderful honey is produced from the flowers.

Traditionally borage was used to drive away sorrow and melancholy. It has well-tried medicinal properties and an infusion makes a soothing treatment for bronchitis and catarrh.

Care
Borage grows best in fertile, well-drained soil and requires a site in full sun.

New plants
Sow seeds in spring or autumn directly into the border.

H To 3m (10ft)
S 60cm (24in)

15–17°C (60–62°F)

Direct sunlight

H 45cm (18in)
S To 45cm (18in)

15–17°C (60–62°F)

Direct sunlight

Calendula officinalis
Pot marigold

The pot marigold is one of the most familiar of the annual herbal flowers. The wild plant can be seen growing all over the Mediterranean region in Europe, on wastelands and cultivated ground. In the wild it has smaller blooms, but centuries of selection has produced varieties with larger flowers. There are now many varieties of this herb, from dwarf to tall, with single but mostly double flowers in all shades from pale orange to deep red-orange. Each bushy plant bears many dozens of flowers and distinctive seed heads, in which the seeds form a tight circular cluster.

The pot marigold often seeds itself, but seeds can be sown in spring, and the plants will be in full flower during summer. Pot marigold really brightens up the herb garden and can be grown equally well in a flower border oran island bed. It looks much more natural grown as an individual plant rather than en masse.

Do not confuse the pot marigold with the other African marigolds, which are listed under Tagetes.

Care
Pot marigolds prefer loam but thrive in most garden soils. They will tolerate dry conditions and require a site in full sun.

New plants
Sow seeds in spring directly into the border.

H & S 30–60cm (12–24in) by 45cm (18in)

18–20°C (65–70°F)

Direct sunlight

Callistephus chinensis
China aster

China asters are useful plants for a bed or border, or in containers, including window boxes. Recent developments have led to a number of useful additions of the dwarf bedding types, and the cultivar 'Milady Dark Rose' is recommended. The rose-coloured double flowers are borne above the dark green foliage. Plants are about 23cm (9in) high, making them ideal bedding plants, especially in areas where wind may cause damage to taller types.

Asters can be affected by various wilt disorders so avoid planting them in the same spot more than once.

Care
China asters like ordinary well-drained soil and an open and sunny site. Avoid overwatering the plants at any stage.

New plants
Sow seed under glass in early spring at a temperature of 16°C (60°F). Use any good seed compost for this purpose, and the subsequent pricking out into boxes. Harden them off in the usual way and plant out into flowering positions in early summer, 15cm (6in) apart.

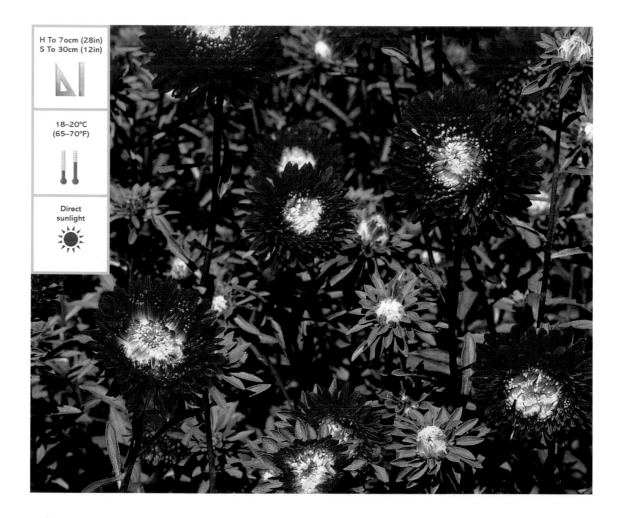

H To 7ocm (28in)
S To 30cm (12in)

18–20°C
(65–70°F)

Direct sunlight

Centaurea cyanus

Bachelor's buttons, Cornflower

The common native cornflower, a hardy annual, is a great favourite, but selection and breeding over many years has led to improved strains for the garden. If you decide to grow this plant, try 'Blue Ball', an attractive blue type. Strong 90cm (36in) stems carry the ball-like flowers well above the leaves, which are narrow and lanceolate in shape. Grow in bold groups near godetias and you will have a beautiful contrast of colour during the summer. They are often grown as cut flowers either in the border or in rows in another part of the garden. 'Red Ball' is another attractive variety.

Care
Cornflowers like ordinary well-drained soil and a sunny location. Give support to very tall types.

New plants
Sow seeds in either autumn or spring; those sown in autumn will make larger plants. Take out drills where the plants are to flower, sow the seed and cover. Thin out subsequent seedlings to 45cm (18in). In very cold areas, protect autumn-sown seedlings from frost.

H To 75cm (30in)
S To 60cm (24in)

16–18°C
(62–64°F)

Direct
sunlight

Cleome spinosa 'Colour Fountain'
Spider plant

This is a very unusual-looking half-hardy annual; the flowers are spider-shaped and scented. 'Colour Fountain' mixture will include shades of rose, carmine, purple, lilac and pink. Stems reach 60–90cm (24–36in) and carry digitate leaves of five to seven lobes. Some spines may be evident on the undersides of these leaves. This is extremely useful as a 'spot' plant to give height to formal bedding schemes. As a border plant, its height will add character, but care should be taken to position it towards the rear in a sunny place.

Care
Spider plants like light, ordinary soil in full sun. Check for aphids on young plants.

New plants
To flower in summer, seed will need to be sown under glass in spring. Use a seed compost and keep the plant at a temperature of 18°C (65°F). Prick out the seedlings into individual pots, 9cm (3.5in) in diameter. Harden off gradually and plant out in late spring.

H To 120cm (48in)
S To 45cm (18in)

18–20°C
(65–70°F)

Direct
sunlight

Carthamus tinctoria
Safflower

Safflower is also known as false saffron, American saffron and dyer's saffron. Beyond its practical value it is also a decorative annual, with spiny leaves and lovely, thistle-like, golden-yellow flower heads.

Safflower is often grown as an ornamental in the herb garden and is a good border plant. Before sowing in spring, look closely at the seeds, which are shiny, white and shell-like. Sow a small patch of the plant, or several patches if you have room. Its flowers will brighten up the garden from summer into autumn.

The golden flowers of safflower are in great demand as a dye and yield both yellow and a pinkish red; these are used mainly for dyeing silk. The flowers are also blended with talc to make rouge and may be dried for winter decorations. They also provide a saffron substitute for colouring food. However, safflower seeds are most valued today as a source of edible oil. This is rich in linoleic acid, which helps to lower blood cholesterol and is widely sold as a health food product.

Care
Safflowers prefer well-drained soil and require a site in full sunlight.

New plants
Propagate from seed in early spring under cover.

Centaurium erythraea
Centaury

Centaury belongs to the gentian family. This is a tiny, delicate-looking plant with bright rose-pink flowers and few leaves. The flowers are very light sensitive and open only on bright days. Its medicinal properties are similar to those of *Gentiana lutea* (yellow gentian).

Centaury is not easy to grow in the garden unless the soil is suitable; a poor, alkaline soil is ideal. Centaury grows well in fine grassland on poor soil.

Centaury is a bitter tonic herb used as a tea to stimulate digestion and reduce fevers, and as a bitter flavouring in certain liqueurs.

Care
Centaury prefers dry, rather poor, alkaline soil and a site in full sun.

New plants
The seed is like dust; it is best surface sown in the autumn where the plants are to grow. This plant self-seeds.

H 60–90cm (24–36in)
S 23cm (9in)

15–17°C (60–62°F)

Direct sunlight

H To 30cm (12in)
S 10cm (4in)

15–17°C (60–62°F)

Direct sunlight

Consolida ambigua
Larkspur

The larkspur, a favourite cottage-garden flower, was once classified as Delphinium. Larkspur flowers are usually a rich blue or purple, but there are selections of pinks and white.

Although the plant is adaptable, it requires well-drained soil.

The larkspur makes an excellent cut flower, and the dried stems and seed heads are particularly decorative. Although in times past it was used medicinally, larkspur is a poisonous plant. Its chief use is as an insecticide. The juice of the leaves makes a good blue ink or colouring for paper.

Care
Larkspur prefers fertile, well-drained soil and a site in full sun.

New plants
In milder climates, seed it in the autumn for early summer flowering and in spring for colour later in the year. Scatter seed in a border or island bed through other plantings in a random fashion.

Warning All parts of this plant are poisonous.

Coreopsis tinctoria
Tickseed

This native North American plant is often known as tickseed. In some catalogues it is listed under the genus Calliopsis. *C. tinctoria* is available only in seed form from herb and wildflower specialists and is very different from the horticultural varieties. It bears jewel-like flower heads of intense golden-yellow and rich reds. Each plant is well branched and blooms abundantly over a long period.

The plants grow very bushy, with wiry stems: trim them early in the season to encourage them to bush out and prevent them from growing too tall. In the border or island bed, plant them either singly as bright colourful accents or in groups. Wild unselected seed gives a good variety of flower colour. Coreopsis looks stunning with a backdrop of grey and silver foliage.

Coreopsis is an important natural dye plant. The flowers yield yellows, oranges, bronzes and reds.

Care
Coreopsis will thrive in most well-drained, fertile soils and requires a site in full sun.

New plants
Sow coreopsis where it is to grow or raise it in small plugs or cellular trays and plant out in spring.

H To 90cm
(36in)
S 23cm(9in)

15–17°C
(60–62°F)

Direct
sunlight

H 60–90cm
(24–36in)
S 30cm (12in)

15–17°C
(60–62°F)

Direct
sunlight

Digitalis
Foxglove

The stately foxglove is one of our best-loved and most elegant wildflowers. It often occurs in large, dramatic stands in woodland clearings, sometimes in profusion on roadsides, and even on rocky hillsides.

This flower can be grown in a wide range of situations in the garden and is very adaptable, but it looks best in a fairly shady position, against a dark background created by trees or shrubs. Foxgloves always look stunning, whether planted in large stands or growing singly as graceful specimens.

There are many species of foxglove that are worth growing in the garden. The yellow foxglove is *D. grandiflora*, but *D. lutea* also bears lemon-yellow flowers, and both of these are perennial, unlike *D. purpurea*, which

is biennial, so it will not flower until its second year of growth. Another attractive species is *D. ferruginea*, which has spires of pale orange and brown-and-white flowers in mid-summer.

Care
Foxgloves prefer well-drained, moisture-retaining loam to light sandy soil. They require partial shade or shade.

New plants
Sow seeds in late summer; self-seeds.

Warning This plant is poisonous.

H 90cm–120cm
(36–48in)
S 30cm (12in)

16–18°C
(62–64°F)

Partial
shade

Eschscholzia californica
California poppy

California poppy is a brilliantly colourful flower. There are many garden forms available in a range of beautiful colours from crimson, through orange-red to pink-cream and shades of yellow; some have double flowers like 'Ballerina'. The soft grey-green foliage is a perfect foil for the bright blooms.

This plant will survive even the toughest conditions of poor soil and drought. In a mild climate sow seed in early autumn to flower early the following year. Sow the seeds in drifts to obtain the full impact of these dazzling poppies. The ideal habitat is gravel or any situation where the soil is poor and light and receives maximum sun.

In mild climates the California poppy readily self-seeds.

The juice of the plant, which is mildly narcotic, was used by North American Indians as a toothache remedy. Spanish settlers in California used it to make a hair oil.

Care
California poppies prefer poor, sandy, well-drained soil and a site in full sun.

New plants
Sow seeds in spring or autumn; self-seeds.

H 30–60cm
(12–24in)
S 15cm (6in)

18–20°C
(65–70°F)

Direct
sunlight

Helianthus annuus 'Sungold'
Sunflower

So many people grow the giant types of this hardy annual that it is often forgotten that a number of the same sunflowers have dwarf counterparts.

'Sungold', only 60cm (24in) tall, can have a worthy place in any border as long as it can benefit from a sunny position. The beautiful double golden-yellow blooms can be up to 15cm (6in) across, and almost ball-shaped. The short stems and longish leaves feel coarse to the touch and the leaves have toothed margins. More showy when grown in groups, they are best suited to the front of a bed.

Care
Check carefully for slug damage at germination time.

New plants
Sow seed directly into the ground where they are to flower, putting three seeds to a station. When germination is complete, discard the two weakest seedlings, leaving only the strongest. Spacing should be 30cm (12in).

H To 60cm (24in)
S 15cm (6in)

16–18°C
(62–64°F)

Direct sunlight

Iberis amara

Bitter Candytuft

Many gardeners will recall the hardy annual candytuft as among the first plants that they grew in a small plot as children. Still very popular, this strongly aromatic annual looks good along the edge of a well-used pathway where its scent can be appreciated. Use it also in bold drifts towards the front of a border.

Umbrella-shaped flowers form in clusters up to 5cm (2in) across, on stems 15–38cm (6–15in) high, from early summer to autumn. The colours are purple, rose-red and white. Leaves are green, lanceolate and slender-pointed, and may be smothered by the profusion of blooms. As flowering is quick from seed, successive sowings will help to prolong the season of flowering.

Care

This plant prefers ordinary or poor soil and a sunny situation. Keep removing dead flowers.

New plants

Sow thinly in spring where they are to flower. Seedlings should be thinned to 15cm (6in) spacing. It is essential to carry out this process to avoid overcrowding.

H To 30cm (12in)
S 23cm (9in)

18–20°C
(65–70°F)

Direct
sunlight

Lavatera trimestris 'Silver Cup'

Mallow

Mallows have long been grown for their attractive free-flowering effects. The annual cultivar 'Silver Cup' recommended here is one of a number of new hybrids. Glowing pink blooms 7.5–10cm (3–4in) in diameter are freely produced on stems 60–70cm (24–28in) high and spreading to 75cm (30 in). This plant is a member of the hollyhock family, and its leaves are green, ovate and lobed. Flowers grow from the leaf axils and are trumpet-shaped, almost satin in texture, and very pleasing to the eye. Apart from their use in the perennial border, try them towards the back of an annual border.

Care

Mallows like ordinary soil in a sunny and sheltered spot. Give plants plenty of space.

New plants

Sow seed directly where plants are to flower, in autumn or spring, and cover lightly. Thin out the seedlings of either sowing during late spring to 45cm (18in) intervals. The strong low branching habit of this plant requires no staking.

Lobelia erinus 'Colour Cascade Mixed'

Lobelia

Probably one of the most widely grown half-hardy annuals, lobelia is very versatile. It includes many shades of blue, rose, red, mauve and white eyed flowers, which continue to appear until cut down by autumn frosts.

Although best results are obtained from planting in sunny positions, lobelias also succeed in partial shade.

Care

Lobelia prefer ordinary well-cultivated soil. Keep the plants watered in dry weather and fed at intervals.

New plants

These tender annuals need to be sown in heat in late winter or early spring to obtain maximum results. Sow the small seeds very thinly on the surface of a moistened compost seed mixture and do not cover. Germinate in a temperature of 18–21°C (65–70°F). Water carefully to avoid disturbance. Prick out as soon as the seedlings can be handled. Grow on in cooler conditions when established and harden off to plant out when risk of frost has passed.

H To 75cm (30in)
S 45cm (18in)

15–17°C (60–62°F)

Direct sunlight

H 15cm (6in)
S 30cm (12in)

15–17°C (60–62°F)

Sun or partial shade

Matthiola incana 'Giant Imperial Mixed'

Gillyflower, Stock

Stocks must be one of the most popular scented annuals. En masse this fragrance can be overpowering, however, so do not overplant. The 'Giant Imperial mixture' always provides reliable flowers with a high percentage of doubles. Stems 38–50cm (15–20in) tall carry a profusion of pink, white, lilac, purple and crimson spikes of flowers from early summer onwards. Grey-green soft narrow leaves are formed under the flower heads and give a pleasing and attractive contrast.

Care

Stock will tolerate most soils, but they should preferably be alkaline. It requires a sunny position, but tolerates partial shade. Kill caterpillars at once.

New plants

Sow seed for summer flowering during the early spring under glass at a temperature of 13°C (55°F). Use a loam-based compost for sowing and pricking out seedlings. Grow on at a lower temperature and harden off before planting out 23cm (9in) apart.

H To 50cm (20in)
S to 30cm (12in)

18–20°C
(65–70°F)

Direct
sunlight

Nemophila menziesii, Nemophila insignis

Baby blue eyes

This is one of the more notable hardy annuals from California. Plants grow to a height of 23cm (9in) and have spreading slender stems on which deeply cut, feathery, light green leaves are carried. Appearing from early summer, the flowers are buttercup-shaped and of a beautiful sky blue with a very striking white centre. Each bloom measures 4cm (1.6in) in diameter. This species will tolerate partial shade; use it where a low planting is required.

Before sowing, fork in organic matter if your soil is on the light side. This will ensure that moisture is retained in hot dry spells so that plants can survive.

Care

Baby blue eyes likes ordinary but moist soil. It requires a site in full sun or partial shade. Water freely during dry weather.

New plants

Sow seeds directly where they are to flower, in early spring. Take out shallow drills and only lightly cover the seed. Thin out seedlings to 15cm (6in) apart. In mild regions, autumn sowings will provide plants for flowering in late spring.

H 23cm (9in)

16–18°C
(62–64°F)

Direct
sunlight

Nicotiana x sanderae 'Nicki Hybrids' F1

Tobacco plant

The Nicki F1 Hybrids are a lovely mixture of colours including red, pink, rose, lime green and white. Individual blooms are up to 6cm (2.4in) long, formed into loose clusters. Stems bearing the flowers carry large oblong leaves of a light green. This strain is dwarf and reaches only about 25cm (10in) in height. The blooms of this free-flowering half-hardy annual are sweetly fragrant. Use as a bedding plant for formal beds or borders, beneath a window, or on a patio or yard where the scent can be appreciated, especially in the evening hours.

Care

Tobacco plant prefers rich, well-drained soil and a site in full sun or partial shade. Do not plant out too early.

New plants

Sow seeds under glass in early spring, in a temperature of 18°C (65°F). Seeds should be scattered thinly on top of prepared pots or trays of a seed compost. Prick out in the usual way. Harden off and plant out in early summer, 23cm (9in) apart.

Nigella sativa

Fennel flower

Fennel flower, or nutmeg flower, is a decorative annual herb closely related to *N. damascena* (love-in-a-mist), but bears paler blue to nearly white flowers. The blooms have a fascinating construction: the globular, horned seed pods are carried above the flowers. The herb is in no way related to fennel.

Fennel flower looks best when grown in a patch or drift, possibly in a rock garden or in an open border. In early spring the seedlings make a brilliant, light green carpet. It self-seeds profusely.

The Romans used the black seeds in cooking. The aromatic nutmeg-scented seeds are valued today as a seasoning in curries and many other dishes, for spreading on bread or cakes, and as a substitute for pepper. The seeds also have some medicinal properties and were employed to treat indigestion. The dried seed heads are highly decorative.

Care

Fennel flower prefers medium to light, well-drained soil and a site in full sun.

New plants

Sow seeds in autumn or spring.

H 38cm (15in)
S 30cm (12in)

15–17°C (60–62°F)

Direct sunlight

H 45cm (18in)
S 15cm (6in)

15–17°C (60–62°F)

Direct sunlight

Oenothera biennis

Evening primrose

Evening primrose is something of a misnomer as, although many species open their flowers at dusk, they are often open for much of the day, especially in cloudy weather. Their wonderful, intense fragrance is most noticeable at night. The tall *O. biennis* is most suited to any dry situation or stony ground, where a selection of evening primroses can be grown.

Evening primrose has recently become an important medicinal herb used in capsules to treat premenstrual syndrome, multiple sclerosis and other conditions. The thick root of the plant has been used as a vegetable.

Care
Evening primrose prefers well-drained soil and a site in full sunlight.

New plants
Sow seeds in late summer; self-seeds.

H To 120cm (48in)
S 45cm (18in)

18–20°C
(65–70°F)

Direct
sunlight

Onopordum acanthium

Scotch Thistle

This magnificent plant has been the national emblem of Scotland since the early 16th century – hence its name.

The plant is biennial. In the first year it produces a large, impressive rosette of leaves a few centimetres above the ground. In the second year it reaches its stately proportions, of up to 2.4m (8ft).

This herb requires plenty of space in the garden to self-seed freely, and one specimen alone will provide an architectural and focal point in an area of waste ground or gravel.

The seeds contain an oil that was used in lamps and for cooking. The heads and young stalks, stripped of their rind, can be eaten. A decoction of the flower heads was used to treat baldness and ulcers.

Care

Scotch thistle tolerates most soils but prefers poor, sandy loam. It requires a site in full sun.

New plants

Sow seeds in spring and early summer.

H To 2.4m (8ft)
S 1.2m (4ft)

18–20°C
(65–70°F)

Direct
sunlight

Papaver
Poppy

Of all the many members of the poppy family, the genus Papaver is the largest. The red corn poppy, or Flanders poppy (*Papaver rhoeas*) is immortalized as the Poppy of Remembrance, and is the most common and best loved.

The seeds of the corn poppy can remain viable in the soil for many decades, but the earth must be disturbed or cultivated for the plant to appear. It will not grow well among established thick vegetation. Seed a patch of waste ground for a quick and colourful display, perhaps with other bright cornfield flowers like *Anthemis arvensis* (chamomile) and *Centaurea cyanus* (cornflower).

P. somniferum (opium poppy) is a larger plant. The flowers are big and handsome, in a range of colours with a large dark blotch at the base. Many varieties have been developed with double, peony-like or fringed carnation-like flowers in various shades. The decorative opium poppy self-seeds readily. In some areas it is illegal to grow this plant. This is an invaluable medicinal plant, today utilized in the manufacture of pain-killers such as codeine and morphine.

Care
Poppies will grow in most soils, including chalk. They like a site in full sun.

New plants
Sow seeds in late summer, autumn or early spring; self-seeds.

H To 90cm (36in)
S 23cm (9in)

16–18°C
(62–64°F)

Direct
sunlight

Petunia x hybrida
Petunia

In a good sunny summer, the petunia is second to none for its profusion of colour and versatility of use. Flowers are trumpet-shaped, up to 10cm (4in) across. Leaves and stems will be a mid- to dark green. Leaves vary in size but are usually ovate. The whole plant feels sticky to the touch. Use these petunias for a range of purposes including formal bedding, borders, containers, window boxes and hanging baskets.

Petunias are really half-hardy perennials, but are invariably grown as half-hardy annuals. All petunias love a sunny position and benefit from being grown in a well-cultivated soil. Avoid having the soil over-rich, as this can lead to a lot of growth and few flowers.

Care
Petunias prefer ordinary well-cultivated soil and a sunny location. Remove faded flowers regularly.

New plants
Seeds will need to be sown under glass in early spring. Sow thinly on top of a seed compost in pots or trays. Prick out the seedlings into trays, harden off and plant out in early summer. Spacing will depend on the cultivar you choose.

H To 30cm (12in)
S To 120cm (48in)

16–18°C
(62–64°F)

Direct
sunlight

Phacelia tanacetifolia
Phacelia

Phacelia has recently come to the notice of gardeners as a good green manure crop. It is also a superb beekeeper's plant, being especially attractive to the honeybee.

This plant has the advantage of rapid growth, providing quick ground cover and a shallow, extensive root system that produces a fine soil. Dig in, or prolong its life span by cutting before flowering. Beekeepers should leave the plant to flower over a long period, and it will then self-seed.

Phacelia is extremely decorative. Sow a good-size patch in any area of the garden that you do not intend to use for a few months and wait for a wonderful display of colour.

Care
Phacelia will tolerate most soils, but prefers some moisture.It needs a site in full sun or partial shade.

New plants
Sow seeds in spring after frost; self-seeds. In mild areas phacelia will overwinter as young self-sown seedlings; in colder areas, however, it should be sown anew each year by broadcasting the seeds and raking in. The more thickly it is sown, the lower it will grow.

H To 90cm (36in)
S 30cm (12in)

18–20°C
(65–70°F)

Full sun or
partial shade

Phlox *drummondii* 'Carnival'
Annual phlox

An easy-to-grow, half-hardy annual, *P. drummondii* will give a succession of colour throughout the summer. For a really bright display try the cultivar 'Carnival'; this mixture has pink, rose, salmon, scarlet, blue and violet flowers. The flowers are borne on stems 30cm (12in) high which carry light green lanceolate leaves. Blooms are produced in early summer as dense heads up to 10cm (4in) in diameter; each individual flower is rounded. These plants are ideally suited for low-growing areas of the garden, especially the rock garden.

Care
Phlox like ordinary well-drained soil and an open, sunny site. Dead-head to prolong flowering.

New plants
In spring, sow seeds under glass in a temperature of 16°C (60°F). Use any good growing medium for sowing. Sow the seeds thinly and cover them lightly. Prick out the young seedlings, when large enough to handle, into trays. Harden off and plant out in flowering positions in early summer at 23cm (9in) intervals.

H 30cm (12in)

16–18°C
(62–64°F)

Direct
sunlight

Tagetes erecta 'Orange Jubilee' F1

African marigold

Marigolds are half-hardy annuals and are very reliable. The cultivar 'Orange Jubilee' is no exception. One of a strain of Jubilee types growing to 60cm (24in) tall, they are often referred to as 'hedge forms' because of the dense foliage. 'Orange Jubilee' is an F1 hybrid and, although seeds are relatively expensive, they are worth the extra cost because of the reliable uniformity of flower.

Carnation-shaped double blooms are produced on the almost erect stems of very sturdy plants. The blooms are light orange in colour and individual flowers can be 10cm (4in) in diameter. Foliage, kept below the flowers, is light green and deeply cut. All parts of the plant are very pungent. The plant will look good formally planted with other complementary subjects. Plant out at 30cm (12in) apart.

Care
Marigolds will grow happily in any soil, so long as they are planted in an open and sunny site. Dead-head to prolong flowering.

New plants
Sow seed in spring in containers in a cold frame.

H 60cm (24in)

15–17°C
(60–62°F)

Direct
sunlight

Tropaeolum majus
Nasturtium

The nasturtium, or Indian cress, is among the brightest and most colourful of garden flowers. This decorative herb makes an excellent companion plant for the vegetable garden. The dwarf form looks attractive around shrubs, in the border, or in a container.

The vivid flowers make a colourful decoration for green salads, and the leaves add a peppery flavour. The seeds can be pickled when still green. The nasturtium also has some medicinal properties. The seeds are antibacterial and an infusion of the leaves is used to treat infections of the genito-urinary tract and bronchitis.

Care
This plant prefers dry to moisture-retaining loam and requires a site in full sun or partial shade.

New plants
Propagate by sowing seeds in spring.

H 30cm (12in)
S To 45cm (18in)

18–20°C
(65–70°F)

Full sun or
partial shade

Verbena x hybrida 'Florist Mixed'
Verbena

This half-hardy perennial is invariably grown as a half-hardy annual. The variety 'Florist Mixed' provides a diverse colour range. The stems, 23cm (9in) in height, tend to spread and make a mat. The rainbow shades of the flowers are produced above the foliage, which is dark green – this gives a jewel-like effect. This perennial is very useful as a front plant for window boxes, containers or flower beds and borders.

Plant in a good-size clump to obtain the best and longest effect of flowering. Those for containers and window boxes can be planted out slightly earlier as long as they are in sheltered positions. Spacing should be 23cm (9in) apart.

Care
Verbenas will grow happily in any fertile soil in a sunny position. Water plants freely in very dry weather.

New plants
Sow seeds in pots or trays in early spring under glass. Keep at a temperature of 16°C (60°F). Use any good growing medium. Prick out the young seedlings, as soon as they are ready, into trays. Harden off and plant out into flowering positions in early summer.

H 23cm (9in)

18–20°C (65–70°F)

Direct sunlight

Viola tricolor
Heartsease

Heartsease, or Johnny-jump-up, is a delightful wildflower that blooms continuously all summer and well into the autumn. It readily cross-pollinates with other violas to produce a wide range of colour combinations. Hundreds of varieties of violas and violettas are available from specialized growers and suppliers. This is a delightful small flower for the container gardener, for it can be planted around the edges of the containers to provide long-lasting colour and interest.

Heartsease self-seeds everywhere. It will thrive in the rock garden, in gravelly or sandy areas, and in a border or even a formal herb garden. It enjoys hot sun.

Medicinally it was used as a blood purifier, for fevers, as a gargle, and to treat ulcers and sores. It is fed to racing pigeons as a tonic and blood purifier. The dainty little blooms can be sprinkled on green salads.

Care
Heartsease grows best in fertile to sandy loam. It enjoys a site in full sun.

New plants
Sow seed in spring in containers in a cold frame. This plant self-seeds freely.

H 10–30cm
(4–12in)
S To 20cm (8in)

18–20°C
(65–70°F)

Direct
sunlight

Zinnia elegans 'Hobgoblin Mixed'
Zinnia

The 'Hobgoblin' mixture of this half-hardy annual has a range of colour in shades of red, pink, yellow and gold.

Zinnias make good bushy compact plants. The stems are about 25cm (10in) long and branched. The leaves are ovate, pointed and light green. Both stems and leaves are covered with stiff hairs. These plants are ideal for borders and beds in a bright, sunny situation.

Care
Zinnias will tolerate any ordinary well-drained soil. They require an open, sunny position. Avoid overwatering at any stage.

New plants
As a tender half-hardy annual, this plant will need to be raised from seed under glass in spring. Sow seeds in any good compost that is free-draining. Keep at a temperature of 16°C (60°F). Prick out seedlings into individual peat pots; this will avoid handling the stems at a later date, which can be damaging. Grow on in the usual way and harden off at the end of spring. Plant out carefully in early summer, 23cm (9in) apart.

H 25cm (10in)

15–17°C
(60–62°F)

Direct
sunlight

DIRECTORY

Perennials

Acanthus mollis

Artist's acanthus, Bear's breeches

This attractive, architectural herbaceous perennial has glossy-green foliage. The mauve-pink, foxglove-like flowers are rather sparingly produced on stems 120cm (48in) or higher. As plants can spread as much as 90cm (36in) and have invasive roots, it is advisable not to grow more than one plant in small gardens. Any good fertile soil suits this acanthus, provided it is well-drained. Plant in spring. During the first winter, especially in cold districts, give a mulch of leaf-mould or well-rotted garden compost.

A. spinosus, the spiny bear's breeches, is similar in many respects, except that it has sharp spines at the end of each dark, deeply divided leaf. Each leaf is about 60–90cm (24–36in) long.

Care

Bear's breeches prefer well-drained soil and a sunny position. Protect from frost and drying winds in their first winter.

New plants

Propagate by seed sown in spring in a cold frame, by root cuttings in late autumn or winter, or by division in spring.

H To 120cm (48in)
S 45cm (18in)

18–20°C
(65–70°F)

Direct
sunlight

Achillea millefolium

Yarrow

Yarrow is an aromatic perennial. The attractive foliage is made up of thousands of tiny leaves (hence the name millefolium).

Since it seeds profusely, yarrow must be kept within bounds. Seed heads should be cut off before they ripen and at this stage can be hung up to dry and used in decorative dried arrangements. This plant is a good subject to naturalize in an area of wild grasses.

Yarrow was once used as a wound poultice in ancient times. Many of its common names refer to its ability to stem the flow of blood. It is also valuable as a remedy for fever and as a digestive tonic. A useful dye plant, it produces browns and greens.

Care

Yarrow will tolerate most soils except the very poorest. It requires a site in full sun, although it will tolerate partial shade.

New plants

Sow seeds in spring; divide in spring or autumn; take softwood cuttings in early summer.

H To 60cm (24in) – spreading

16–18°C (62–64°F)

Direct sunlight

Anemone x hybrida

Japanese anemone, Japanese windflower, Windflower

Of all the many anemones, the best-known are the many hybrids of the hardy, herbaceous perennial *Anemone* x *hybrida* (also known as *A. japonica*). These vary in height from 45–120cm (18–48in), and their individual flowers vary in size from 4–6cm (1.6–2.4in) across, each with five or more petals. Each flower has a central boss of yellow stamens. The stems are clothed with vine-like leaves. Their roots are like stiff black leather bootlaces. Choose from the following selection: 'Bressingham Glow', a semi-double rosy red, 45cm (18in) tall; 'Luise Uhink', white, 90cm (36in); 'September Charm', single soft pink, 45cm (18in);

'White Queen', 90–120cm (36–48in); and 'Honorine Jobert', white, 120cm (48in).

Care

Anemones like good ordinary soil. Good drainage is needed and, preferably, a sunny position.

New plants

Propagate by cutting the roots into 4–5cm (1.6–2in) lengths and inserting them in a deep box filled with compost and sand mixture.

H Variable to 120cm (48in)

18–20°C (65–70°F)

Direct sunlight

Aster amellus

Italian aster, Italian starwort

This colourful herbaceous perennial has large solitary flowers with golden-yellow centres and several clusters to each strong branching stem. The grey-green foliage and the stems are rough when handled. These plants form a woody rootstock.

Four varieties to choose from are: 'King George', soft blue-violet 8cm (3in) flowers with golden-yellow centres, introduced seventy years ago; the 60cm (24in) tall 'Nocturne', with lavender-lilac flowers; the large-flowered pink 'Sonia', 60cm (24in); and the compact dwarf aster, 45cm (18in) tall, 'Violet Queen'.

They object to winter wetness and are happiest in a good well-drained retentive soil. They are best planted in spring.

Care
They need retentive well-drained soil in a sunny position. Do not let them have wet roots in winter.

New plants
Propagate by basal cuttings in spring or by division where possible.

H To 60cm (24in)
S 45cm (18in)

16–18°C
(62–64°F)

Direct sunlight

Aster novi-belgii

Michaelmas daisy

Michaelmas daisies are superb herbaceous perennials with large and colourful daisy-like flower heads in September and October. They need to be grown in fertile soil, as they soon exhaust the ground. Position in full sun.

There are many varieties to choose from ; some of these are: 'Carnival' with semi-double, cherry-red flowers 60cm (24in) high; 'Freda Ballard' with semi-double, rich red flowers 90cm (36in) high; and 'Royal Ruby' with semi-double, rich ruby, early flowers 50cm (20in) high.

Dwarf varieties include: 'Jenny' with double red flowers 30cm (12in) high; 'Professor Kippenburg' with clear blue flowers 30cm (12in) high; and 'Snowsprite' with white, late flowers 30cm (12in) high.

Care
These plants need a fertile soil in a sunny position. If mildew attacks, spray flowers with sulphur.

New plants
Propagate these plants by dividing the roots in spring, every three years. Replant only the healthiest pieces.

H To 60cm (24in)
S To 90cm (36in)

18–20°C
(65–70°F)

Direct
sunlight

Astilbe x arendsii
False goat's beard

Astilbes are one of the most decorative hardy herbaceous perennials. The arendsii hybrids vary from white, through pale pink, deep pink, coral and red, to magenta. Not only are they good garden plants, but they also force well under glass in an unheated greenhouse. The foliage varies from light to dark green, with some of purplish and reddish-purple shades. The fluffy panicles of flowers are held on erect stems 60–90cm (24–36in) tall, but dwarf varieties are only 45cm (18in).

They will grow in full sun or partial shade and thrive in most soils. They have a long flowering period and their rigid erect stems do not require staking. There are too many varieties to mention, but all are worth a place in any garden.

Care
These plants require a moist fertile soil and a site in full sunshine, although they will tolerate partial shade. Do not cut old flower stems back before spring.

New plants
Propagate by division in spring. Alternatively, roots may be divided in autumn and potted for forcing or spring planting.

H To 90cm (36in)
S 60cm (24in)

16–18°C
(62–64°F)

Direct
sunlight

Campanula lactiflora
Milky Bellflower

This is a superb herbaceous perennial which will reach a height of 120–150cm (48–60in), and in partial shade may reach 180cm (72in), though it is better in full sun. Its stout stems require staking in windy gardens. The rootstock, although vigorous, fortunately does not rampage in the soil. The rigid stems carry loose or dense panicles of white or pale blue to deep lilac flowers. The stems are clothed with small light green leaves. The flesh-pink 'Loddon Anna' is a lovely form of C. lactiflora, 120–150cm (48–60in) tall. The baby of this species, 'Pouffe', only 25cm (10in) high, is an ideal dwarf plant, with light green foliage forming mounds that are smothered for weeks with lavender-blue flowers during the early and mid-summer months.

Care
Grow in fertile, moisture-retentive soil in sun or partial shade.

New plants
Propagate by division in autumn or early spring.

H To 150cm (60in)

18–20°C (65–70°F)

Direct sunlight

Ceratostigma

Plumbago

This group consists of about eight tender, deciduous perennials and shrubs from eastern Africa and eastern Asia. These plants, commonly known as plumbagoes, are grown for their attractive autumn foliage and pretty, blue flowers. They are excellent for growing in the rock garden or flower border. *C. griffithii* is a low-growing, semi-evergreen plant with deep blue flowers and bright red, autumn foliage that persists well into the winter. After a harsh winter, this plant may not blossom. *C. willmottianum* (Chinese plumbago) is a deciduous shrub that grows about 1m (3ft) high. The blue flowers are produced from mid-summer until autumn when the leaves become stained with red.

Care
Plumbagoes can be grown in mild climates only. They should be planted in the spring, in dry, well-drained soil in a sunny location. In the spring, the old flowering growths should be pruned back.

New plants
These plants may be lifted, separated and replanted in the spring. Cuttings may also be taken in the summer and inserted in very sandy soil outside and covered with a bell jar, or placed in a greenhouse or frame.

H 60–100cm (24–36in)

20–25°C (70–80°F)

Direct sunlight

Chelone obliqua
Turtlehead

This rather strange-looking herbaceous perennial derives its popular name from the unusual shape of its flowers. It is a close relation of the penstemons and is sometimes confused with them. Its dark green leaves are broad to oblong in shape, 5–20cm (2–8in) long, and arranged in pairs, the last two being just below the erect crowded truss of rosy-purple flowers. The square stems are 60–90cm (24–36in) tall. Provided it is given a sunny position in the border, this plant will produce blooms for several weeks in autumn. The flowers are very weather resistant, which is useful in wet seasons. Its roots have a spreading habit.

Care
Chelones prefer fertile well-drained soil and a position in partial shade. They may crowd out less tough growing plants.

New plants
Propagate by seed sown in spring under glass in a temperature of 13–18°C (55–65°F), or in late spring without heat in a cold frame. Also, propagate by division of roots in spring or in late autumn as soon as flowers fade.

Chrysanthemum maximum
Shasta daisy

The Shasta daisy, a native of the Pyrenees, is a must for any herbaceous perennial border. The height varies from 60 to 90cm (24–36in). Flowers are single or double, with plain or fringed petals. Because of the large flat heads, rain and wind can soon knock plants over. Short peasticks should be inserted in the ground before the plants are too advanced.

One of the best-known varieties is 'Esther Read', 45cm (18in) tall, with pure white, fully double flowers. 'Wirral Pride' is a 90cm (36in) beauty with large anemone-centred blooms and another variety is the fully double white-flowered 'Wirral Supreme', 80cm (32in) high. If you prefer a large, fully double, frilly-flowered variety, plant 'Droitwich Beauty', 80–90cm (32–36in) tall. The creamy-yellow 'Mary Stoker' is 80cm (32in) tall.

Care
Shasta daisies like any good fertile soil in a sunny position. Be sure to provide support.

New plants
Propagate by softwood cuttings in summer, or by division in autumn or spring.

H To 90cm (36in)

15–17°C (60–62°F)

Partial shade

H Variable to 90cm (36in)

15–17°C (60–62°F)

Direct sunlight

Convallaria majalis

Lily of the valley

Lily of the valley is still an old-fashioned favourite, popular for its delightful hanging and very fragrant, bell-shaped blooms.

This plant is always at its best grown in drifts, in a woodland setting, but if there are no trees or shrubs to cast shade, a north-facing wall is suitable. The clear white of the flowers and the fresh green foliage look best against a dark background. In ideal conditions the rhizomes will spread rapidly and form a large patch. Plant the crowns well below the surface.

Lily of the valley has for centuries been used medicinally. The flowers are used as a perfume base.

Care

Lily of the valley prefers humus-rich, well-drained, moisture retaining to dry soil. It requires a site in shade or partial shade.

New plants

Divide in the autumn or after flowering.

Warning All parts of this plant are poisonous.

H 30cm (12in)
S 15cm (6in)

16–18°C
(62–64°F)

Shade or
partial shade

Crocosmia masonorum

Montbretia

This South African cormous plant has sword-like leaves with pronounced centre spines, and grows to 75cm (30in) tall. The flowers are bright orange, 2.5cm (1in) long, and the plant will give a succession of blooms from mid-summer.

These plants can be invasive; confine them by planting in a bottomless container sunk into the ground. The plants need a well-drained soil, but keep it moist during summer droughts. The flowers are often used for cutting; if they are left on the plants, remove them as soon as they die. Cut off dead leaves before the new ones appear in spring. They are normally pest- and disease-free.

Care

Montbretia likes well-drained sandy soil and a sunny location. Plant 7.5cm (3in) deep.

New plants

The corms should be planted in spring, 7.5cm (3in) deep and 15cm (6in) apart, in a sunny position. Corms should be lifted every few years; divide after flowering and before new growth appears.

H 75cm
(30in)

18–20°C
(65–70°F)

Direct
sunlight

Cynara scolymus
Globe artichoke

The globe artichoke was grown by both the ancient Greeks and Romans. The edible part of the plant is the large flower head, harvested before the flower opens. It is also an architectural foliage plant for the garden, where it makes a dramatic display in a mixed border or island bed. The purple, thistlelike blooms are enclosed by scales that curve back on the upper rows, giving the flower heads their characteristic appearance. The flowers attract bees and insects.

The artichoke is not very hardy, and needs a light, sandy, very well-drained soil to ensure it survives the winter. For vegetable production it requires a moisture-retentive soil. Protect the crowns from hard frosts.

At the end of the season, the dried heads are beautiful, and if cut when the plant is in bloom, the rich colour of the flower will be preserved. The artichoke is also a valuable medicinal plant. The leaf and root are used to treat the liver and in digestive tonics.

Care
Globe artichokes are hardiest when they are grown on well-drained, dry soils. They require a site in full sun.

New plants
Sow seeds in spring; divide suckers in late spring.

H To 180cm (72in)
S 90cm (36in)

16–18°C
(62–64°F)

Direct
sunlight

Delphinium elatum
Delphinium

These are hardy herbaceous perennials, well-known for decorating borders with spires of flowers during June and July. The true species is seldom grown, and the forms now cultivated are *D. elatum* (large-flowered type) and *D. belladonna* types.

The elatum plants develop long, upright spires of flowers on plants up to 240cm (96in) high, although dwarf forms, such as 'Baby Doll' and 'Blue Fountains', and medium-height forms, like 'Blue Nile' and 'Cressida', are available.

Derived from the elatum are the belladonna varieties. They are smaller at between 100–150cm

(40–60in) high. They have a lax, graceful habit and beautifully cupped florets.

Care
These summer- and autumn-flowering plants prefer deep rich, well-drained and moisture-retentive soil. They require a site in full sun. Avoid cold, wet soils and plant in spring.

New plants
Propagate delphiniums by division or by cuttings rooted in a cold frame in spring.

H 240cm (96in)

18–20°C
(65–70°F)

Direct
sunlight

Dianthus 'Dynasty'
Pink

Dynasty is a range of double-flowered dianthus with flowers that have the appearance of mini-carnations. The plants bear well-branched, strong-stemmed, upright flowers that are lightly scented, and come in four colours – a rich purple, a velvety red, 'Rose Lace' which is a lovely deep rose with a fine white outer edge, and 'White Blush', which has white flowers with a rose-pink blush that fades as the flower matures.

Pinks have long been favourites with cottage gardeners but their charm and scent means that they are a good addition to any garden.

Care
Frost-tolerant and requiring minimal maintenance, Dynasty dianthus like full sun and well-drained, neutral soil.

New plants
Propagate perennial dianthus from cuttings in summer.

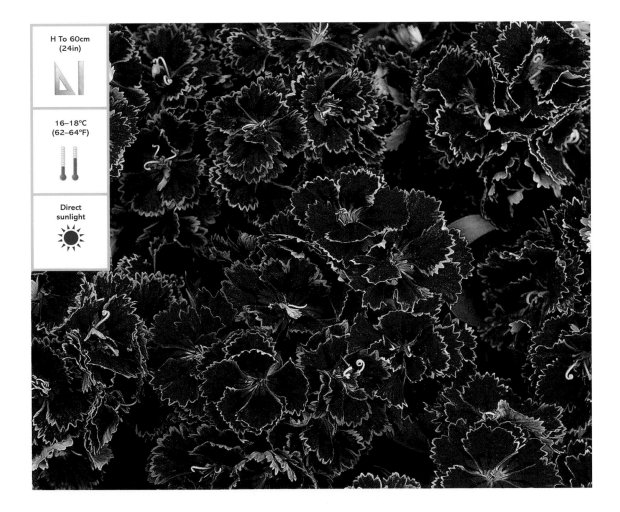

H To 60cm
(24in)

16–18°C
(62–64°F)

Direct
sunlight

Dictamnus purpureus
Burning bush

Burning bush is so called because the flowers give off an inflammable vapour in hot, dry conditions. The whole plant is also highly aromatic, reminiscent of lemon peel and balsam.

Burning bush is a magnificent-looking plant that should have a lightly shaded position in a border, with a fairly dry loam soil. Grow it with other plants that enjoy similar conditions, such as *Filipendula vulgaris* (dropwort), *Linum perenne* (perennial flax) and *Pulsatilla vulgaris* (pasqueflower).

The plant has been used medicinally in the past but is little valued today. The scented leaves provide a tea substitute.

Care
Burning bush likes well-drained alkaline loam and a site in full sun, although it will tolerate partial shade.

New plants
Sow seeds fresh in late summer; divide plants in spring; take root cuttings in late autumn or early winter.

H 60–90cm
(24–36in)
S 45cm (18in)

15–17°C
(60–62°F)

Direct
sunlight

Echinacea purpurea
Purple coneflower

The purple coneflower is a colourful native of the North American plains and is the species most often grown in gardens.

E. purpurea is a dramatic flower which can be planted in small drifts in the border to stunning effect. The species E. angustifolia is more drought tolerant than E. purpurea, which requires some soil moisture over a hot summer. All members of this genus are hardy in the right soil conditions and will stand heat and humidity.

Echinacea is a valuable medicinal plant. The dried root was extensively used by the Plains Indians in North America, especially the Sioux, to treat septicaemia, snakebites and rabies. It is thought to be a blood purifier and have antibiotic properties. Today its most important use is to enhance the immune system.

Care
Purple coneflowers like fertile, well-drained soil which retains some moisture in summer. They require a site in full sun or light shade.

New plants
Sow seeds in late spring or early summer at 21°C (70°F); divide plants in spring or autumn.

H To 60cm (24in)
S 23cm (9in)

16–18°C
(62–64°F)

Direct sunlight

Echinops humilis 'Taplow Blue'
Globe thistle

Globe thistles are herbaceous perennials with round drumstick heads in varying tones of blue. They are coarse growing with stout rough wiry stems and deeply cut, greyish, spiny foliage, woolly beneath. Bees are especially attracted to the globular flowers. The flower heads can be dried for winter decoration. The variety 'Taplow Blue' is 150cm (60in) tall with dark blue globular flowers that have a metallic steely lustre. A variety with a slightly richer blue is 'Veitch's Blue'.

These hardy herbaceous perennials can be grown successfully in the poorest of soils, whether sand or chalk, but should be well-drained.

Care
Globe thistles will grow happily in any soil, so long as it is situated in full sun. Provide a good depth of soil, as the thong-like roots of this plant are very penetrating.

New plants
Propagate by root cuttings in late autumn or winter, or by division in autumn or spring.

H 150cm (60in)

18–20°C (65–70°F)

Direct sunlight

Fuchsia

Fuchsia

One of the most widely cultivated plants in the world, fuchsias are beautiful and exotic. There are thousands of different types of this plant, which was originally bred from a handful of wild species found in Mexico, the West Indies and New Zealand.

Colours vary from pinks, purples, whites and reds to sober or flashy multicoloured mixtures. Several (for example *Fuchsia magellanica*) can even be grown as hedges.

Fuchsias basically divide into the hardy types that can be left outside all year, the bushy or upright and tender kind for pots, and the dangling, trailing ones for hanging baskets.

All fuchsia flowers have three parts: the upper tube; the sepals beneath that often point out like wings; and the corolla (the petals) – the skirt-like growth underneath the sepals. Each can be a different colour in some varieties.

Care
Most fuchsias require little care, apart from a spring pruning to generate new growth. Situate in full sun.

New plants
Grow new young plants in rich, moist compost and pinch out the young shoots regularly to encourage bushiness. These can be used as cuttings.

Geranium maculatum

Spotted Cranesbill

Spotted cranesbill is a pretty woodland flower of North America with clear lilac-blue flowers that appear in late spring, earlier than those of most other hardy geraniums. The Latin name, maculatum, means 'spotted' and refers to the pale spots that develop on the leaves. The decorative foliage turns to beautiful autumn colours of fawn, orange and red.

Although it is a woodland plant, cranesbill will grow in the garden and forms a dense ground cover. It has thick rhizomes, which in time form good-size clumps. This plant requires some moisture to do well, but it will also withstand a certain amount of drought. It readily self-seeds, and the seed pods, constructed like catapults, eject their contents when ripe.

The powdered rhizome is used medicinally for a range of ailments, including diarrhoea and sore throats, and to stop bleeding.

Care
Spotted cranesbill prefers humus-rich, moisture-retaining loam and a site in full sun or partial shade.

New plants
Sow seeds or divide plants in the autumn.

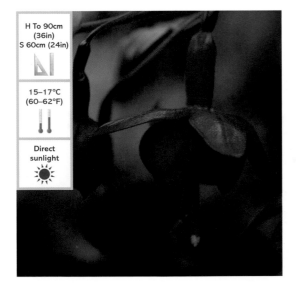

H To 90cm
(36in)
S 60cm (24in)

15–17°C
(60–62°F)

Direct
sunlight

H To 60cm
(24in)
S 45cm (18in)

15–17°C
(60–62°F)

Direct
sunlight

Gypsophila paniculata
Baby's breath

The flower heads of this perennial are a mass of small feathery flowers, white or pink. The glaucous leaves are also small. The branching flower heads are used by flower arrangers to add a light cloud effect to floral arrangements. *G. paniculata* 'Bristol Fairy' is the best double form, at 90cm (36in) tall.

As gypsophilas are deep-rooted, the ground must be well prepared before planting; it should be double dug. To do this, take out the first spit or spade's depth of soil, break up the bottom spit with a fork and fill up with the next top spit. Also enrich the ground with well-rotted

farmyard manure or well-rotted garden compost. Provided they have full sun and well-drained soil, gypsophilas should be no trouble.

Care
Baby's breath prefers well-drained, preferably limy, soil and a sunny location. Insert a few peasticks for support.

New plants
Propagate 'Bristol Fairy' by taking softwood cuttings in late spring to very early summer.

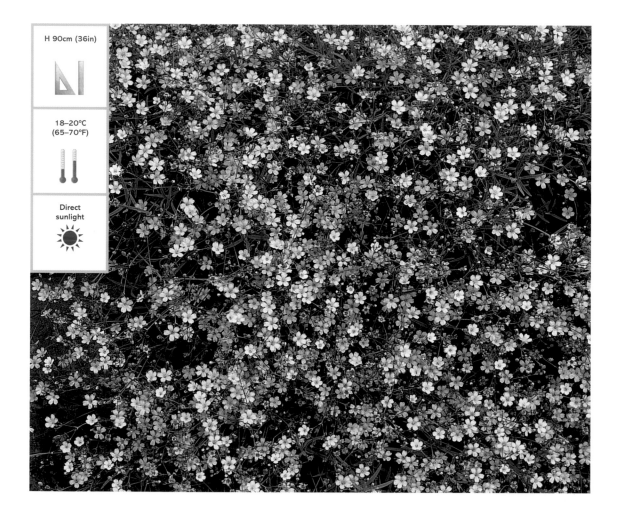

H 90cm (36in)

18–20°C
(65–70°F)

Direct
sunlight

Hemerocallis fulva
Daylily

The daylily is so called because each flower opens for only a day, but the plant has blooms in succession over a long period. It enjoys a certain amount of moisture and, if the soil is damp enough through the summer, will grow naturally with grass, to make an exotic flowering meadow.

H. fulva is a vigorous plant that needs space to spread. Grown alone among shrubs in light shade or full sun, or beside a stream, it can make a spectacular sight. Other daylilies are less vigorous.

The Chinese considered the flower buds of this plant a delicacy. Other parts of the daylily, however, are thought to be potentially toxic. The root was used in traditional Chinese medicine for various ailments, and is believed to be antibacterial.

Care
Day lilies like fertile, moist or moisture-retaining soil and must be situated in full sun or partial shade.

New plants
Divide in spring or autumn.

H 90cm–120cm
(36–48in)
S 30cm (12in)

16–18°C
(62–64°F)

Direct
sunlight

95

Kniphofia

Red-hot poker

Kniphofias are herbaceous perennials that will come through most winters. To ensure their safety, tie the foliage into a kind of wigwam in winter, to keep the crowns dry. The flowers are carried on stout stems. One beauty is 'Little Maid' about 60cm (24in) tall, with attractive creamy flower spikes. *K. galpinii* 'Bressingham Seedlings' produce orange spikes, 45–90cm (18–36in) tall.

Kniphofias require a fairly rich soil with ample humus such as rotted manure or garden compost. After clumps have been divided, do not allow them to dry out before or after planting. A mulch of rotted manure or garden compost should be given annually in spring, otherwise they can remain untouched for several years. Plant them three or four to the square metre (square yard).

Care

These early summer- to autumn-flowering plants prefer rich, retentive well-drained soil in a site in full sun. Protect crowns during winter.

New plants

Propagate by division in spring.

H To 90cm (36in)

18–20°C
(65–70°F)

Direct
sunlight

Lonicera periclymenum
Wild honeysuckle

There are more than 100 species and varieties of the honeysuckle. The wild honeysuckle, or woodbine, grows in woods and hedgerows, filling the summer air with its seductive perfume

Honeysuckle also looks attractive if it is planted in the more formal herb garden or vegetable garden, it may be grown on a surrounding fence or to make a fragrant arbour, often a feature of old gardens.

Over time perhaps a dozen of the many species of honeysuckle have been used in medicine. A decoction or ointment from the flowering herb is now used mainly externally, to treat skin infections.

Care
Honeysuckle grows best in a soil enriched with compost or leaf mould. The ground should be well prepared before planting. Old wood can be thinned out to maintain a good-looking plant.

New plants
Take woody cuttings in early autumn; layer in late summer; sow seeds in autumn (stratify).

Warning The berries are very poisonous.

To 9.1 m (30 ft) – climbing

18–20°C (65–70°F)

Direct sunlight

Lupinus polyphyllus
Lupin

Lupins enjoy sun and well-drained soil. Take care to avoid lime and heavy wet clay soils. Before planting, see that the ground is well cultivated, with an ample supply of well-rotted farmyard manure or garden compost. On well-drained soils, plant in autumn; otherwise, wait until spring.

With established plants, restrict the number of flower spikes to between five and seven, when stems are about 30cm (12in) high. Give a light spraying of plain water in the evening during dry springs. As a rule, staking is not necessary. Named varieties can be obtained, but the Russell hybrids have a good mixture of colours and vary in height from 90 to 120cm (36–48in). In very windy gardens, sow the dwarf 'Lulu' lupin. This is only 60cm (24in) tall.

Care
These early summer-flowering plants prefer light sandy loam in full sun. Remove faded flower heads to prevent them forming seeds which will take strength from the plant.

New plants
Propagate by basal cuttings in early spring, when 7.5–10cm (3–4 in) long; insert in a cold frame.

H To 120cm (48in)

18–20°C (65–70°F)

Direct sunlight

Lysimachia nummularia
Creeping Jenny

Creeping Jenny has many other old country names, the most common of which is moneywort, referring to the round, pennylike leaves, and possibly to the golden flowers that resemble cascading coins.

This is a decorative ground-cover plant for moist or wet ground that gets some shade. It thrives if grown in a woodland-edge or pond-edge site, and provides early green ground cover followed by profuse, brilliant gold flowers. A cover of leaf mould mulch, about 15cm (6in) deep, every autumn will do it good. Allow this plant space to spread. In warmer climates creeping Jenny can become too rampant for the small garden.

An old medicinal herb, it was supposed to have many virtues and was used as a compress for wounds.

Care
Creeping Jenny prefers moist, humus-rich loam. It requires a site in shade or partial shade.

New plants
Divide in spring.

Paeonia officinalis
Peony

The peony is a robust shrub that was developed for its beautiful blooms. Most of the forms of peony now available bear spectacular double flowers in many colourful shades.

Essentially a plant of the woodland edge, the peony looks its best associated with trees and shrubs. Grow it as a specimen plant and give it space and a rich, woodland soil, with plenty of leaf mould. The peony will withstand periods of drought in summer, drawing on reserves in its thick rootstock.

P. officinalis, sometimes called the apothecaries' peony, is an early cultivated plant, named by the ancient Greeks after Paen, the physician to the gods. The plant is still valued medicinally by the Chinese.

Care
Peonies prefer humus-rich, moisture-retaining but well-drained soil and a site in partial shade or full sun (avoid early-morning sun).

New plants
Sow seeds in autumn; divide roots with a bud in early autumn.

Warning The flowers are poisonous.

H Very low growing (trailing)

15–17°C (60–62°F)

Shade or partial shade

H To 90cm (36in)

15–17°C (60–62°F)

Direct sunlight

Passiflora incarnata

Passionflower

Passionflower must be among the most exotic of all flowers. It makes a superb dense cover for sheds or fences, and can also be trained to grow up through a large tree. When mature the plant produces many flowers, followed by edible fruits.

In a small garden or patio, growth will be restricted. The plant can be grown successfully in a container. *P. incarnata* will not stand temperatures below freezing; the species *P. caerulea* is a hardier plant and more suitable for northern climates.

Far from arousing 'passion', as its name suggests, *P. incarnata* is in fact a sedative and tranquilizer with a mild narcotic effect. It is still much used in European herbal medicine.

Care

Passionflowers prefer fertile and well-drained soil and a site in partial shade.

New plants

Sow seeds in spring, pre-soak; keep moist.

H 9.1m (30ft)–
climbing

18–20°C
(65–70°F)

Partial
shade

Phlomis russeliana

Jerusalem sage

This handsome weed-smothering plant, or ground cover, has large, rough, puckered, heart-shaped, felty, sage-like grey-green leaves. Among the foliage, stout flower spikes, 75–90cm (30–36in) high, carry whorls of soft rich yellow hooded flowers in early summer to mid-summer. The attractive seedheads can be used successfully in flower arrangements, whether green or dried. Phlomis will grow in ordinary garden soil in an open, sunny location.

Care

These summer-flowering plants like a well-drained ordinary soil and a sunny location. Plant phlomis against a suitable background, such as a red-leaved Japanese maple.

New plants

Propagation of this plant is by seed, cuttings or division, in spring or autumn.

H To 90cm (36in)

18–20°C
(65–70°F)

Direct
sunlight

Polemonium caeruleum
Jacob's ladder

Jacob's ladder is so called because of the ladderlike formation of its bright green leaves. This is a cottage flower that has been grown for many centuries in country gardens.

Jacob's ladder requires moisture in the soil to flourish and grows well in partially shaded areas. It associates well with water, and with trees and shrubs. For a long flowering, cut down the stems before they go to seed so that more will be produced. One stem will be more than adequate for self-seeding, since seeds are produced in abundance.

In times past the herb was used to treat fevers, headaches, epilepsy and nervous complaints.

Care
Jacob's ladder prefers humus-rich, moist to moisture-retaining, calcareous loam. It requires a site in full sun, although it will tolerate partial shade.

New plants
Sow seeds in spring or autumn; divide roots in spring; self-seeds.

H 60–90cm (24–36in)
S 30cm (12in)

18–20°C (65–70°F)

Direct sunlight

Physostegia virginiana
Obedient plant

This hardy herbaceous perennial is called the obedient plant because its flowers have hinged stalks and can be moved from side to side and remain as altered on their square stems. The long, narrow, dark green, glossy leaves are toothed and grow in four columns. The dull rose-pink flowers terminate the square tapering spikes, 45–105cm (18–42in) tall. They bloom from summer to autumn, until the frosts spoil their beauty. Physostegia has vigorous stoloniferous rootstocks that spread underground.

There are several good varieties: 'Rose Bouquet' has pinkish-mauve trumpet flowers; 'Summer Snow' is pure white and about 75cm (30in) high; and 'Vivid' bears rose-crimson flowers on stalks 30–45cm (12–18in) tall.

Care
This late summer flowering plant likes any good fertile soil and a site in sun or partial shade. Give this plant sufficient moisture during dry summer weather.

New plants
Sow seeds in spring or autumn; divide roots in spring. This plant self-seeds. Propagate by division in spring or by root cuttings in winter.

H To 105cm (42in)

15–17°C
(60–62°F)

Indirect
sunlight

Primula vulgaris
Primrose

The primrose is one of the earliest spring flowers. It once grew in great profusion in the wild, but many of its natural habitats have now been destroyed. Primroses enjoy a rich soil with moisture and a thick mulch of leaf mould. They always look their best associated with woodland and can be successfully naturalized in woodland and partial shade or in grass which should be left uncut until after seeding in mid-summer. Primrose stems curve over to the ground when the seeds are ripe. If seed is sown when fresh, germination will occur during the autumn; otherwise, it needs the winter cold to stimulate germination.

The plant has medicinal properties similar to those of the cowslip. The flowers can be candied.

Care
Primroses prefer humus-rich, moisture-retaining loam and a site in shade or partial shade.

New plants
Sow seeds as soon as they ripen or stratify. Divide in the autumn.

H To 20cm (8in)
S 20cm (8in)

18–20°C
(65–70°F)

Shade or
partial shade

Rudbeckia fulgida
Coneflower

One of the most useful border and cut flowers in late summer and autumn. Erect 60cm (24in) stems rise from leafy clumps, displaying several large golden-yellow, daisy-like flowers with short blackish-purple central discs or cones, hence the name coneflower. The narrow leaves are rather rough to handle. Other garden forms of *R. fulgida* are the free-flowering *R. f. deamii*, 90cm (36in) tall, and 'Goldsturm' which, above its bushy growth, has stems 60cm (24in) tall carrying chrome-yellow flowers with dark brown cones. Rudbeckias make good cut flowers and blend very well with *Aster amellus* 'King George'.

Care
This late summer- and autumn-flowering plant prefers moist fertile soil in a site in full sun. Do not let plants dry out during the summer.

New plants
Propagate by dividing the plants in autumn or spring.

H To 90cm (36in)

16–18°C
(62–64°F)

Direct
sunlight

Salvia x superba
Salvia

Each erect 90cm (36in) stem carries branching spikes of violet-purple flowers with reddish-brown bracts (modified leaves). There are also dwarf varieties, such as 'Lubeca' with masses of violet-blue flowers, 75cm (30in) high and 'East Friesland', violet-purple and only 45cm (18in) tall. These salvias look well when planted on their own.

Salvias are both fully hardy and perennial. They will grow in any good fertile soil or on chalk but they dislike dry soils and should not be allowed to dry out. Some form of support should be given, such as peasticks pushed in around the plants to allow them to grow through.

Care
Salvias like any good fertile soil and a site in full sun. Support the tall varieties.

New plants
Propagate salvias by division in spring or autumn.

H To 90cm (36in)

18–20°C
(65–70°F)

Direct
sunlight

Schizostylis coccinea

Crimson flag

This rhizomatous herbaceous perennial from South Africa grows freely in most soils. In South Africa, it grows near water and needs ample moisture to flower. It has long stems, 60–75cm (24–30in) or more and pretty, cup-shaped flowers open in a star-like fashion, not unlike small gladiolus flowers. *S. coccinea* has rich crimson blooms about 4cm (1½in) across. The varieties 'Major' and 'Gigantea' are even brighter and larger. 'Mrs Hegarty' is pale pink and 'Sunrise' has large pink flowers. The flowering stems are excellent for cutting.

The rhizomatous roots need to be lifted, divided and replanted every few years to keep them thriving. A spring mulch of peat or well-rotted garden compost will help to retain moisture around the plants.

Care
This early autumn-flowering plant likes any moist fertile soil situated in full sun. Be sure to keep plants moist.

New plants
Propagate by division in spring, always leaving four to six shoots on each portion.

H To 75cm (30in)

16–18°C
(62–64°F)

Direct
sunlight

Sedum spectabile 'Autumn Joy'

Ice plant

The name ice plant probably originated because this species has glaucous glistening foliage. The leaves are opposite or in threes and clasp stout erect stems 30–60cm (12–24in) high. Above these stems are borne flat, plate-like, unbranched flowers. *S. spectabile* has pale pink blooms. The varieties 'Carmen' and 'Meteor' are a deeper pink, and 'Brilliant' is a deep rose-pink. 'Autumn Joy' is at first pale rose, gradually changing to a beautiful salmon-pink. Later it turns a beautiful brown to give a pleasant winter display. The flat flower heads will be besieged by bees.

These border perennials can be grown with the minimum of attention.

Care
Grow these late summer-/autumn-flowering sedums in well-drained soil situated in full sun. Give these plants room – about five to a square metre.

New plants
Propagate these plants by taking stem cuttings in mid-summer and rooting in sandy soil in a cold fame, or by division in late summer or autumn.

H To 60cm (24in)

18–20°C
(65–70°F)

Direct
sunlight

Solidago 'Goldenmosa'
Aaron's rod, Golden rod

Golden rod, at one time, meant some small, yellow, one-sided sprays at the top of tall, stout, hairy stems. Today, there is a much larger selection of these herbaceous perennials. The variety 'Goldenmosa' has pretty frothy flowers and miniature heads of the original golden rod, similar to mimosa. The rough hairy flower spikes are 75cm (30in) tall.

Two smaller varieties are the 45cm (18in) 'Cloth of Gold' with deep yellow flowers and 'Golden Thumb' with clear yellow flowers on 30cm (12in) stems, which produces neat little bushes ideal for the front of the border.

These vigorous plants will thrive in any good soil which is well supplied with nutrients. A sunny location or one in partial shade will suit them equally well.

Care
Grow this late summer-flowering plant in good ordinary soil in sun or partial shade. Apply humus to taller varieties.

New plants
Propagate all varieties by division in spring.

Viola odorata
Sweet Violet

This lovely flower has always been the harbinger of spring. Every garden, however small it is, should have sweet violets growing in some shady corner, perhaps around a tree, among shrubs, or at the edge of woodland where there is shade during the hottest part of the day. Violets will also establish themselves in short grass. They need some moisture and enjoy a woodland-type soil with plenty of leaf mould. A few plants will soon spread in suitable conditions. Sweet violets look best growing with other wild woodland herbs, such as primroses, oxlips, hellebores, wild strawberries and lungwort. Grow violets in earthenware containers, which can be brought into the house in winter and placed on a windowsill.

Medicinally sweet violet is valued for its soothing expectorant properties in the treatment of respiratory disorders, including bronchitis. It alleviates and cools hot swellings, and is also mildly sedative. The flowers are extensively used in perfumery. In Britain the flowers were cooked with meat and game and can be candied.

Care
Violets like moisture-retaining to moist, humus-rich, alkaline soil and a site in shade or partial shade.

New plants
Sow seeds in autumn; divide plants in late winter or early spring.

H 75cm (30in)

16–18°C (62–64°F)

Direct sunlight

H to 15cm (6in), spreading

15–17°C (60–62°F)

Partial shade or shade

DIRECTORY

Bulbs, Corms & Tubers

Allium cristophii
Onion

This bulbous perennial produces ribbed stems and strap-shaped, grey-green basal leaves with stiff marginal hairs that decline as its flowers form. In early summer, it bears umbels that are 25–30cm (10–12in) in diameter, and contain up to 100 star-shaped fuchsia flowers with a metallic sheen.

This plant's flowerheads dry particularly well.

Care
This allium prefers full sun and humusy, well-drained soil.

New plants
Propagate from seed in spring. Remove offsets in autumn.

Allium giganteum
Onion

Originally from Iran, Afghanistan and Central Asia, where it grows on lower mountain slopes, this is a bulb that prefers a well-drained and sunny situation. Tall and densely flowered it is impressive, but is not quite the giant that its name suggests. The flower stems are 120–150cm (48–60in) tall with broad basal leaves which are withered at flowering time. The flower is a dense orb formed of many purple flowers about the size of a grapefruit.

Care
Giant alliums like fertile, sandy to moist loam and a site in full sun or light shade.

New plants
Propagate from seed in spring. Remove offsets in autumn.

H 25–30cm (10–12in)
S 30cm (12in)

15–17°C (60–62°F)

Direct sunlight

H 120–150cm (48–60in)
S 30cm (12in

15–17°C (60–62°F)

Direct sunlight

Alstroemeria aurantiaca

Lily of the Incas, Peruvian lily

This tuberous-rooted plant has twisted blue-grey leaves and grows to a height of 90cm (36in). Borne on leafy stems, the flowers are trumpet-shaped in orange-red with red veins.

Plant the tubers in spring. Cover with a mulch of compost or well-rotted manure in spring. As they grow, support to prevent them being blown over. Dead-head plants to encourage more blooms. In autumn cut stems down to the ground.

Watch for slugs and caterpillars, using an insecticide if necessary. When the plant shows yellow mottling and distorted growth, destroy it – this is a virus disease.

Care

Peruvian lilies prefer well-drained fertile soil and a sunny, sheltered site. Avoid damaging the roots. Protect in winter.

New plants

Plant tubers 10–15cm (4–6in) deep. Sow seed in spring in a cold frame and plant out a year later. In spring the plants can be divided, but take care not to disturb the roots unduly. Sometimes the plant will not produce any stems, leaves or flowers during the first season but, once established, it can be left for years.

H 90cm (36in)

16–18°C
(62–64°F)

Direct
sunlight

Amaryllis belladonna
Belladonna lily

This bulbous plant has strap-like leaves, lasting from late winter through to mid-summer. After the leaves die down, flower stems appear and grow to a height of 75cm (30in). The trumpet-shaped fragrant pink or white flowers vary from three to 12 on a stem.

Dead-head the flowers as they fade; remove leaves and stems as they die.

Care
Belladonna lily likes a well-drained soil and a sunny, sheltered position. Keep moist when transplanting.

New plants
Plant the bulbs in summer in a warm, sheltered situation in well-drained soil. Bulbs can be divided in summer and should be replanted immediately.

H 75cm (30in)

18–20°C
(65–70°F)

Direct sunlight

Crinum
Crinum

The large trumpet-shaped flowers of crinums bring an exotic touch to gardens in late summer and early autumn. This is a stately plant that is hardy down to around –5°C (23°F). However, to ensure that they come through cold winters, it is essential to plant crinums in a warm position – preferably at the base of a warm wall or similar protected place.

The large 15cm (6in) bulbs produce strong stems at the top of which emerge the 15cm (6in) wide, 12.5cm (5in) long, sweetly smelling, lily-like flowers. The six petals have a satiny look to them. Each bulb will produce three to four stems each one bearing up to 10 flowers. Plant three or more bulbs closely together for a dramatic display. Once planted the bulbs should be left undisturbed for several years if possible as they may take a long time to settle in again.

Care
Crinum needs a well-drained, but moisture-retentive, humus-rich soil and a sheltered, warm, sunny position.

New plants
Plants can be propagated by dividing the clumps in spring.

Crocus spp.
Crocus

Crocus corms are generally known as bulbs but they are actually solid stems from which a bud containing the leaves and flower emerges. Although regarded as spring-flowering plants, some species of crocus flower in the autumn and others in winter. So by planting a range of species you could have flowers for almost nine months!

All produce funnel-shaped, six-petalled flowers on short stems low down to the ground. The flowers, which open and close with sunlight, are available in a wide range of colours, often with a colour contrast between the inner and outer petals and often with contrasting markings. In some species the flowers open out wide but others remain goblet shaped. Many species produce scented flowers.

The narrow, grass-like foliage usually has a central white or grey stripe and grows longer as the flowers fade. Some of the autumn-flowering species produce leaves after the flowers, but in the spring-flowering types they appear together.

Care
Crocuses grow well in any well-drained soil and prefer a site in sun or light shade. Try to keep corms dry during their summer dormancy.

New plants
Plants are propagated by removing offsets when the leaves die back.

H 90cm (36in)
S 60cm (24in)

15–17°C
(60–62°F)

Direct sunlight

H 20cm (8in)

15–17°C
(60–62°F)

Direct sunlight

Cyclamen
Cyclamen

The hardy cyclamen make delightful ground cover plants under trees and shrubs and, by choosing species carefully, you can have flowers from late summer through to late spring. They are fabulous garden plants often growing where other bulbs will not. The elegant flowers in shades of pink, crimson, mauve and white have gracefully reflexed petals and are held above the heart-shaped or rounded leaves. The latter often have fine white or silver marbling which adds to the overall attraction. Because the foliage lasts for some time it helps sustain a long period of interest. Cyclamen are perfect for naturalising among trees and shrubs, or for growing on rock gardens and in containers.

Care
Cyclamen needs well-drained but moist, humus-rich soil and a site in partial shade. Top dress the soil annually with leafmould or compost and add a little bonemeal.

New plants
Unlike other plants the tubers of cyclamen cannot be cut into sections, so the only way to increase your stock is to buy new tubers. Most species do self-seed quite reliably and dense stands of plants can be built up in this way.

H Various

12–18°C
(55–65°F)

Partial
hade

Eranthis hyemalis
Winter aconite

This European tuberous-rooted plant grows to a height of 10cm (4in) with a spread of 7.5cm (3in). The leaves are pale green and deeply cut. The bright yellow flowers appear in late winter but in mild winters the flowers may start blooming in mid-winter. The flowers are about 2.5cm (1in) across and look like buttercups but with a collar of pale green leaves just below the flower.

Plant tubers in a well-drained soil that is moist throughout the year – a heavy loam is ideal. Grow them in either sun or light shade. If sooty eruptions occur on the plant, destroy it to stop the spread of smut disease.

Care
Aconites prefer a well-drained heavy soil and a site in sun or partial shade. Keep soil moist in spring.

New plants
To propagate, lift the eranthis when the leaves die down. Break or cut the tubers into sections and replant these immediately, at least 7.5cm (3in) apart. Seed can be sown in spring and kept in a cold frame; transplant in two years and flowering will start after another year.

H 10cm (4in)
S 7.5cm (3in)

16–18°C
(62–64°F)

Direct
sunlight

Fritillaria imperialis
Crown Imperial

This bulbous plant grows up to 90cm (36in) tall, with a centre stem on which is carried a series of narrow, pointed, glossy leaves to half the total height. The top half of this stem carries a circle of large beautiful drooping flowers about 5cm (2in) long with a crown of leaves. The range of bloom colour is yellow, orange and red.

   The bulb should be planted in autumn in a rich well-drained soil in shade, preferably where it can be left undisturbed. Handle bulbs carefully and do not let them dry out. Plant the bulb on its side to stop water getting into the hollow crown and rotting the bulb. In heavy soil, a handful of coarse sand around the bulb will speed drainage. Cut the stems down when they die off in summer. Seed will not produce flowering bulbs for six years.

Care
Crown imperials like a well-drained soil in full sun or partial shade. Do not bruise or dry the bulb.

New plants
To propagate by the quickest method, use offsets taken from the parent bulb in late summer; plant in a nursery bed for two years, then transplant them to the flowering position.

H 90cm (36in)

15–17°C
(60–62°F)

Full sun or
partial shade

Galanthus nivalis

Snowdrop

Snowdrop leaves are flat, sword-shaped and often blue-green in colour. The flowers are either single or double, in white with green markings on the inner petals, and can be as long as 2.5cm (1in). Snowdrops flower from mid-winter onwards. One variety of this bulbous plant flowers in late autumn, before the leaves appear. They can grow up to 20cm (8in) tall in rich soil and in partial shade.

The bulbs should be planted 10cm (4in) deep in heavy soil, or 15cm (6in) deep in light soil, in autumn. The soil should be moist but well-drained. Move bulbs after they have finished flowering, while the soil is moist. Seed may take five years to bloom, so it is better to split clusters of bulbs and spread them out. Take care when lifting not to damage the roots or to let them dry out.

Care
Snowdrops like rich, well-drained soil and partial shade. Leave bulbs undisturbed for several years for improved flowering.

New plants
Propagate by splitting clumps and replanting as soon as flowering is over.

H 20cm (8in)

15–17°C
(60–62°F)

Partial
shade

Hyacinthus spp.
Hyacinth

Although hyacinths make excellent garden plants, they are more commonly grown indoors for winter or early spring displays on windowsills, table tops or just about anywhere else their colourful, fragrant flowers can be enjoyed.

The plants of the Dutch hyacinth *H. orientalis* – with their erect flowerheads densely packed with up to 60 flowers, and fleshy, strap-like foliage – can look perfect for up to three weeks in the right conditions. They are excellent for growing in containers outside – but ensure the compost doesn't get frosted right through – in informal borders and more formal bedding schemes.

Providing the bulbs are planted in good soil with plenty of added humus they can be left in the ground all year. However, the display in the subsequent years may not be as good and when used in formal bedding schemes this may be a disadvantage. Instead it may be a better idea to let the foliage die down, then lift the bulbs and store them in dry compost in a cool, dry place until it is time to replant in autumn.

Care
Hyacinths can be grown in any humus-rich soil. They will tolerate light shade but prefer direct sunlight.

New plants
Remove offsets in summer while the bulb is dormant.

H To 30cm (12in)

15–17°C
(60–62°F)

Direct
sunlight

Ipheion uniflorum
Spring starflower

These bulbous plants are noted for their grass-like, sea-green leaves and star-shaped flowers. The plants grow only 20cm (8in) tall, with spring flowers 5cm (2in) wide. The white to deep lavender-blue blooms are scented.

Bulbs should be planted in autumn. Plants should be kept weeded. When leaves and flower stems die back in summer, they should be removed. Position plants in full sun in well-drained soil. The bulbs are increased by bulblets. The plants should be lifted in autumn, divided, and replanted at once. Do this every two or three years to keep the plants free-flowering and healthy. Make sure bulbs do not dry out or become wet during transplanting,

and keep the time out of the soil to the minimum. Ipheions are generally trouble-free provided the soil is kept free-draining.

Care
Spring starflowers like ordinary soil with good drainage and a site in full sun. Do not let bulbs dry out or become wet when planting or transplanting.

New plants
Propagate these flowers by dividing bulbs (including offsets) in autumn.

H 20cm (8in)

15–17°C
(60–62°F)

Direct
sunlight

Iris reticulata

Iris

These hardy Asian bulbous plants have a net of fibres around the outside of the bulb and grass-like tubular leaves that are dark green with a paler tip. They are early flowering; some start at mid-winter and others follow successively through to spring. The flowers are often 7.5cm (3in) wide, in lemon-yellow and blue. These plants are small and ideal for the rock garden; they rarely grow more than 15cm (6in) tall.

Plant them in a light, well-drained chalky soil. If the ground is heavy, the bulb may not flower after the first year. Give each bulb a covering of 5–7.5cm (2–3in) of soil. They do best when planted in autumn.

Care

Irises prefer light, well-drained, limy soil and a site in light shade or sun. Do not plant in heavy moist soil. After flowering give a liquid feed every four weeks until the bulb dies back.

New plants

Propagate by dividing congested clumps of bulbs in the autumn.

H 15cm (6in)

18–20°C
(65–70°F)

Direct
sunlight

Lilium

Lily

True lilies belong to the genus Lilium; they include many popular species and varieties available for the garden.

The madonna lily, which has been grown in gardens for centuries, is one of the most beautiful. The simple white blooms look their best against the dark background of a hedge. Plant them among lower-growing shrubby herbs that shade the soil and keep it cool.

L. martagon (martagon lily or purple turk's cap) has purple flowers that give off their scent at night. This is a hardy lily that enjoys a free-draining soil with lime in full sun or partial shade. The martagon lily looks especially good growing among shrubby plants or in the shade of trees. It seeds itself freely; the bulbs should be planted deep, as this lily produces roots on its lower stem.

Care
Most lilies, with the exception of the madonna lily, enjoy deep planting. Bury the bulb up to 20cm (8in) deep. For best results the soil must be well drained so that there is no risk of waterlogging in winter. They respond to humus-rich soil and potash feed (wood ash is a good source).

New plants
Plant bulbs in the autumn; sow seeds in spring or autumn.

H 90cm–180cm
(36–72in)

18–20°C
(65–70°F)

Direct
sunlight

Narcissus spp.

Narcissus, Daffodil

The genus Narcissus is enormous and highly varied in both size and flower form, ranging from tiny 10cm (4in) dwarf types to traditional, tall garden varieties of 60cm (24in) high. This makes daffodils indispensable and highly versatile plants.

Most daffodils flower in spring, although a few of the earlier ones will start flowering in late winter. The flower colours range from white to shades of yellow and orange-red or pink as well as bicolours. There are singles as well as double-flowered forms.

There are choices for the rock garden, producing informal swathes in grass and on banks, in formal beds and borders – tall ones up to 60cm (24in) for the middle of borders, dwarf forms reaching no more than 10cm (4in) for the front – as well as for growing in containers.

To make classification of all the various species and cultivars easier, Narcissi are split into 13 carefully ordered divisions.

Care

Daffodils will grow in any well-drained soil in a sunny position. However, most will tolerate light shade.

New plants

Remove offsets as the leaves die down in late spring or in early autumn as you plant the bulbs.

H Variable to
60cm (24in)

18–20°C
(65–70°F)

Direct
sunlight

Nerine bowdenii

Nerine

Nerine bowdenii, a half-hardy bulbous plant from South Africa, is sufficiently hardy to withstand most winters in the temperate zone. It will grow to a height of 60cm (24in). The blooms open in autumn, with up to eight flowers in each cluster. The clusters are 15cm (6in) across, usually rose or deep pink, but there is also a white form. The mid-green leaves are narrow and strap-like.

The bulbs should be planted in either late summer or early spring, in an ordinary well-drained soil and in a sunny position. The bulbs are placed just under the surface or, if the soil is light, they can be set deeper – as much as 10cm (4in). Where there are bulbs near the surface, they should be covered with a thick layer of bracken, leaf-mould or compost to protect them against frost. They can be lifted in spring, divided and replanted to encourage larger looms. Watch for mealy bugs and treat them with pesticide.

Care
This plant likes ordinary well-drained soil and a sunny position. Keep moist when growing.

New plants
Propagate by dividing clumps when dormant in summer.

H 60cm (24in)

16–18°C
(62–64°F)

Direct
sunlight

Tulipa
Tulip

Tulips are bulbous plants that are so well-known that they do not need description. In addition to the many types created through selection and hybridization, there are other species that are also worth growing. These include *Tulipa clusiana* (the lady tulip), *T. kaufmanniana* (the water-lily tulip), *T. griegii* and *T. tarda*.

Cross-bred types include Single Early and Double Early forms, which can be planted in flower borders for spring flowering. Other forms include Mendels, Triumph, Darwins, Cottage, Rembrandt and Parrot types.

Plant the bulbs in late autumn, in slightly alkaline soil and full sunlight. Remove the flowers after they fade, but leave the stems and leaves attached to the bulb. If the space is needed for planting summer-flowering plants, dig up the bulbs – complete with stems and leaves – and replant them into a trench in a remote position.

Care
Tulips prefer a slightly chalky soil and a site in full sunlight. Dead-head the plants to build up the bulbs for the following year.

New plants
Propagate by removing offsets in summer.

H Variable to
60cm (24in)

18–20°C
(65–70°F)

Direct
sunlight

Glossary

Annual A plant that completes its cycle of germination from setting seed through dying in a single growing season.

Biennial A plant requiring two growing seasons to flower and seed.
Bract A leaf at base of flower stalk or flower head.
Bulb A plant storage organ, usually formed underground, containing the following year's growth buds.

Calyx Usually green, outer part of a flower, formed from the sepals, that encases the petals in bud.
Corm A swollen stem base that acts as a storage organ, similar to a bulb.
Crown The part of a herbaceous plant from where new stems are produced.
Cultivar A man-made or cultivated variety, produced by hybridization.
Cutting A section of a plant removed for propagation.

Division The splitting of a plant clump into various sections containing roots and shoots; normally done when the plant is dormant, for purposes of propagating or reinvigorating the plant.
Double flowers Applied to a flower head or bloom having more petals than the original species.

Floret One of the individual flowers that make up the head of a composite flower, such as a dahlia.
Flower head A mass of small flowers that appear as one flower.
Force (-ing) A method of promoting early flowering or fruiting, usually via artificial heat and light.

Half-hardy A plant that withstands low temperatures but not freezing.
Hardy A plant that tolerates year-round conditions in temperate climates, including normal frost, without protection.

Herbaceous A non-woody plant that dies down to its rootstock in winter.
Hybrid A plant resulting from crossing two different species.

Inflorescence A group or arrangement of flowers on a stem, such as panicles and racemes.

Layering A method of pinning a stem to the ground and inducing it to form roots, thereby propagating a separate plant.

Mulch A layer of organic or inorganic material added to the surface of the soil to retain moisture, help suppress weeds and gradually improve fertility.

Node The point at which a leaf grows from the stem.

Offset A plant that is reproduced naturally from the base of the parent plant.

Perennial A plant that lives for longer than two seasons.

Raceme A long, unbranched flower stem.
Rhizome An underground, often creeping, stem acting as a storage organ, from which roots and shoots grow.
Rootball The roots together with the soil adhering to them when a plant is lifted, e.g. for transplanting.

Sepals The green outer parts of a flower, collectively forming the calyx.
Single flowers Applied to a flower that has the normal number of petals for its species, such as a daisy.

Type Used to refer to an original plant species.

Variety A variant of a plant species, arising either naturally or as a result of selection.

Index